ARE YOU A FIRST TIME PARENT?

DISCOVER WHAT YOU NEED TO KNOW TO
HAVE A MORE ENJOYABLE AND WELL-
INFORMED TRANSITION INTO
MOTHERHOOD

HENRIETTA MULLINS

CONTENTS

INTRODUCTION

Are you a first-time mother? Do you want to be more prepared when your baby finally arrives? Do you want to learn about all the different things you can expect after childbirth?

Being a first-time parent is a beautiful experience, but it can also be a little nerve-wracking. To enjoy parenthood the way it's supposed to be, without feeling overwhelmed or uncertain, you need a little preparation. This is a special period of your life, and you need to enjoy every second of it without any worry. If you want to do all this, then this, "Are You A First-Time Parent? Discover What You Need to Know to Have a More Enjoyable and Well-Informed Transition into Motherhood," is a must-read.

In this book, I will provide all the information you need to ensure that you are absolutely prepared for motherhood and know what you have to do. All the nervous energy and doubts you might have as a first-time mother will be addressed in this book so that you can be stronger, more positive, and confident. This book has all the information you need for the first 18 months after your baby is born, including information about breastfeeding, sleep and cry techniques, tips for maintaining your mental health, taking care of your physical well-being, and much more.

How do I know all these things? My name is Henrietta Mullins, and I am a happy and proud mother of four children, aged 17, 13, 11, and six years. I know firsthand what the main struggles a first-time mother faces. After my first pregnancy, I wish I had had a brilliant book to guide me on what to expect and how to prepare myself. Every pregnancy is unique, and the joys of motherhood are genuinely irreplaceable. However, after my first pregnancy, I was worried, nervous, and had plenty of doubts about what I was and was not supposed to do. If you feel this way, you don't have to worry because this book will be your guide and best friend.

If you are in a happy state of mind, it will help your newborn. All the chaotic energy you felt and any apprehensions about motherhood will soon go away if you know what to expect. After all, preparation is the best way to deal with any change.

I've designed and written this book to equip you with all the information you need to start motherhood on a positive note. Reading through this book will enable you to hold on to this magical time in your life, filled with incredible happiness. All the memories you make from now on will stay with you forever and will be a source of unlimited joy and happiness. All your doubts will finally go away, and you will be left feeling absolute pleasure that you introduced new life to this world.

After my first pregnancy, I discovered several simple

secrets and tips that helped ease the transition into motherhood. I realized that my struggles were not just me, but shared by many other expectant mothers who could benefit from this information. I started to share my experiences and tips with my friends, relatives, and acquaintances. I was thrilled to learn that these helped them, too. It was then I realized that I should share this information with more people. This is the same information and tricks I will unveil in this book.

I promise, with my help and guidance, you'll be fully equipped with the knowledge and need-to-know information required to understand what you can expect and how to prepare yourself for being a new parent. I will also teach you about certain things you should avoid during motherhood. All this information will make your first-time experience less daunting and more enjoyable and heartwarming. You will also feel confident about your skills as a new mother. Whenever in doubt, you can refer to all the information within this book. All the tips and tricks in this book are incredibly easy and straightforward to follow. They're practical, easy to implement, and you won't have to make any drastic changes.

If you are not well-prepared and informed about how your life changes after childbirth and what you can expect while caring for your little one and yourself, it can take away the joy of motherhood. I don't want this to happen to you. Have you heard the saying, "We rise by lifting others?"

Many new mothers are afraid to ask for help. To make things easier for you, I have shared a variety of tried and tested tips and strategies I know will come in handy. Together, you and I will make sure this time in your life is as enjoyable and memorable as possible. We're in this together, and I'm here to help.

Let's start as we discover the wonders of motherhood and how to create a loving, nurturing, and safe environment for you, your baby, and your family.

1

AFTER BIRTH NEED-TO-KNOWS

I'm expecting my first baby in just a few weeks. I can't believe all the changes that are happening in my body. After I have the baby, how long will it be before I feel "normal" again? Is there anything I have to look out for or worry about when it comes to healing after giving birth?

- Patricia

Congratulations, new mama! Your body just performed a miracle; one of the most remarkable things it can ever do - grow, sustain, and give birth to new life. The joy of motherhood is unlike any other. After patiently waiting for nine months, your bundle of joy is finally home. The excitement of holding your newborn baby isn't comparable to anything else you will ever experience. In the coming weeks and months, most of your time, energy, and attention will be dedicated to your little one. However, you should not forget about yourself in this process. Remember, your body experienced a significant change. It will take some time for it to get back to your usual self.

During the first few days after the birth of your baby, a lot happens. You will experience several physical and emotional changes. You will need to prepare yourself for constant feeding sessions and barely any sleep. Your baby will soon become the centre of your universe; that is a lot to get accustomed to, compared to your life before pregnancy and birth.

Your delivery might have been easy, painful, or a C-section birth. Your labour may have lasted for a few hours or even days. Regardless of what the delivery was like, your body experienced a trauma, and it needs time for recovery. Postpartum recovery isn't quick, and it takes more than a few weeks. Therefore, prepare yourself to take care of your body in the following months as you look after yourself.

Some women might feel recovered within 6 to 8 weeks,

while others can take a while longer. There will be instances when you feel like your body has turned against you, but be patient. You might have some expectations, but your body really cannot follow such timelines. In this section, you will learn about some simple things you should prepare yourself for after your birth.

Bleeding and After-Pains

Immediately after you bring your baby into the world, your uterus starts contracting to expel any remaining blood and tissue. This vaginal discharge is known as lochia. NHS states it usually lasts until your baby is 12 weeks old. Vaginal bleeding is common for the first couple of days after delivery, and it will be bright red. You might also notice some clots that are the size of small tangerines. Even if this seems scary, don't worry because it's perfectly normal. You can use soft sanitary pads to regulate the flow.

If, however, you have a high temperature of over 38C, the bleeding gets unusually heavier, the bleeding smells a bit foul to you, and you have increased tummy and perineum (the area between your vagina and anus) pain call your GP, health visitor or midwife immediately. You may possibly have an infection or something like postpartum haemorrhage that needs emergency care, so the earlier you are checked out by a specialist, the better.

After a few weeks, the bleeding will slowly decrease, and the colour of the discharge changes from bright red to pink, brown, until it becomes clear. The discharge should have a fleshy smell to it and shouldn't be putrid. If you notice the discharge is bright red or has any clots a few weeks after the birth, then it's a sign you need some more rest. All this is your body's way of telling you to get the much-needed rest it needs.

After-pains are as common as bleeding. Pushing a baby out of your body is no small feat, and it is physically tiring and draining for the body. Any after-pains or cramps are coming from contractions of the uterus. They are uncomfortable but normal. After-pains and cramps usually peak on the second or third day after childbirth. The intensity of these after-pains will slowly reduce and can last anywhere between 7-10 days.

To reduce these pains, you might be prescribed some paracetamol or another painkiller. Follow your midwife or doctor's orders and take the medicines in prescribed doses. Research shows that the same simple relaxation and breathing techniques used during labour can also help alleviate these unpleasant cramps. Another simple method to reduce after-pains is to breastfeed your baby frequently. Try, too, to walk around as much as possible after the delivery. Don't restrict yourself to the bed unless bed rest was prescribed.

Lacerations

To facilitate the birth of the baby, you might have had a procedure known as an episiotomy. An episiotomy is a surgical incision that helps elongate your vaginal opening to enable childbirth. The lacerations from this surgery and any accompanying pain tend to vary from one person to another. It's usually caused due to the swelling of the tissue surrounding the vagina and the incision itself. Typically, any discomfort is significantly higher on the second or third day after delivery. Still, it isn't easy to predict how long this discomfort lasts. Some women don't experience any pain, while others experience a constant dull ache. All of this eventually goes away once your body starts to heal itself.

You can use an ice pack, a cooling pad, or pain-relieving spray to reduce any swelling or pain near the perineum and the vagina. Always wash your hands thoroughly before and after you clean the vaginal area. Whenever you pass pee or have a bowel movement, clean your stitches. To do this, you can squirt some warm water using a peri bottle (also known as a perineal irrigation bottle) or a similar apparatus. After this, gently pat dry the area with a clean tissue. If you experience any burning sensation in this area when you urinate, lightly squirt some warm water for relief and cleanliness.

Here is a simple exercise you can use to reduce this discomfort and promote the healing of any lacerations. Whenever you sit, irrespective of whether it is on the bed or the chair, position yourself squarely. Slowly tighten the muscles in the perineum, buttocks, and thighs. Do this gently, and don't exert a lot of pressure. Hold and release a few times. This exercise helps reduce the pressure on the stitches and promotes healing.

Changes in the Uterus

Another physical change after you deliver your baby is how your uterus acts and feels. Immediately after delivering your baby, your uterus will weigh around two pounds for the next few days. If you feel right below your navel, you might even be able to make out your uterus, since it's a little swollen after you give birth. At this point, it's probably about the size of a grapefruit.

When your baby was in your womb, the placenta was

attached to the walls of your uterus. After your baby is born, the placenta detaches from the uterus. The blood vessels shared between your uterus and the placenta open up and start to bleed into the uterine cavity. In response, your uterus contracts to help prevent it from filling up with blood.

As you can imagine, this can be a little uncomfortable. But the good news is that there are some ways to reduce the pain of this process, as well as things you can do to help the uterus heal quickly.

You can help this process along with breastfeeding. Oxytocin, a hormone released when you are breastfeeding, helps discourage uterine bleeding and haemorrhaging; in addition to being known as the "love hormone," oxytocin sparks bonding feelings, and emotional attachments, which reduces stress. This can also contribute to creating a pleasant healing environment for you, including your uterus.

Another technique you can follow is to gently massage your uterus for a couple of days after your delivery. You can do it yourself or seek help from your partner or a nurse. They just need to place one hand on your lower belly, where your uterus is located and rub in a circular motion around it. It will help to stimulate contractions and make your uterus firm and soothe you.

A lot of new moms worry about their expanded uterus size, but there is no need. Your body is a miracle machine and performs most of its internal healing on its own. In most cases, you don't need any external help to contact your uterus; however, if you feel any discomfort, your midwife, health visitor or even your gynaecologist can suggest additional medication. It will ease your pain, as well as help your uterus come back to normal. Before you know it, your uterus will slowly shrink in size and return to its usual size and weight. This process can take up to 6 weeks, but it isn't anything you should be worried about, as it is a normal part of childbirth. If you experience any discomfort, gently massage your uterus to ease the pain. If the pain increases or doesn't reduce, consult your health visitor or midwife. They may suggest some exercises that can help ease the transition.

How to Manage Bowel Movements

It might not sound pretty, but there are three things your body undergoes while birthing. First comes your baby, then the placenta, and finally, your first bowel movement. I know the first poop is not equivalent to delivering a baby, but it can be scary. You might have endured some tearing, stitches, or undergone a C-section. All this, coupled with weakened pelvic floor muscles, a rectum pushed to its limit, and ricocheting hormones in the body can take a toll on your bowel movements. However, it is a common phenomenon, and almost all new mothers go through it.

The first poop after childbirth is seldom easy and almost always painful. The idea of pushing something else out of your body isn't appealing. However, you can take specific steps to reduce this fear and manage any pain or discomfort you experience. Start with a stool softener. The hospital or birthing centre will usually provide you with some, but you can ask for one if they don't. It isn't the same as stimulant laxatives, which affect your milk production. Stool softeners are safe for breastfeeding mothers, so you can rely on them when the going gets tough. Make sure you consume foods rich in fibre and stay thoroughly hydrated to stimulate your first bowel movement.

Constipation is a common issue for most new mothers and can last for up to three weeks after childbirth. Another tip to ease any discomfort is to use a toilet footstool while using the toilet. Place your feet on the toilet stool to raise your knees. Rest your elbows on your knees and concentrate on your breathing. Breathe in slowly and exhale slowly. Gently push while you do this, and the bowel movement comes more naturally.

A 4-week long study by The Ohio State University Wexner Medical Center showed that 71% of the participants experienced faster bowel movements when they simply used a footstool. Toilet footstools help position your body to a natural squatting position; the right position to effectively pass bowel movements. Even in the UK, toilets themselves are higher than average. When sitting on a toilet without a footstool it creates a bend in the rectum that makes it more difficult to pass bowel – toilet footstools straighten that bend in the rectum.

As a new mother, one of your responsibilities is to track your baby's bowel movements. Keep track of your bowel movements too. You don't have to make elaborate or detailed notes. In the crazy rush and excitement of becoming a mum, you might forget to take care of your needs. You would probably think it was just a day, but before you realize it, it could end up being four days since your last bowel movement, which isn't okay. Postpartum constipation is not just uncomfortable but can be exceedingly painful if left unchecked. It could escalate into more severe and painful conditions such as haemorrhoids or anal fissures. Since prevention is always better than cure, it is best to take care of yourself.

Varicose Veins

Varicose veins are large, swollen blood vessels on the lower part of your body, usually the legs. Some women notice them near the rectum or even the vulva. Varicose veins are quite visible during pregnancy and often go away after childbirth. These distinctive purplish lumps might look a little scary, but they are usually harmless.

During pregnancy, your body produces additional blood to support the fetus. This extra blood pumping through your veins increases your blood vessels' strain that works against gravity to supply blood throughout your body and then pump it back into your heart. These blood vessels are already working against gravity, and the increased supply worsens this strain and results in varicose veins.

There are some tips you can use to remedy varicose veins. The simplest thing to do is to keep blood flowing in your body. Move whenever possible, and don't sit or stand in place for too long. Don't overexert yourself, but a little additional movement reduces this strain on the blood vessels. Don't wear uncomfortable clothes, such as tight-fitting shoes, heels, socks with elastic tops, and tight belts.

If you dress comfortably for a while longer, it helps to reduce the occurrence of varicose veins. It might not sound sexy, but wearing compression stockings is a good idea. It counteracts the downward pressure on your abdomen and offers additional upward support for the veins in your legs. NHS recommends to wear compression stockings during the day and at night take them off and continue this routine for however long you need to wear it. But I suggest telling your health visitor or GP before wearing it, just so they can monitor your progress and give you personal feedback.

Always sleep on your left side after pregnancy to reduce the pressure on the major blood vessels and to enhance circulation in your body. There is also a relationship between varicose veins and body weight. Many women gain anywhere between 20-35 pounds during pregnancy, so a little weight loss can help reduce varicose veins.

Don't forget your daily dose of vitamins and avoid any sort of physical strain. Even though pregnancy is one of the happiest moments of your life, it is entirely stressful for your body. Acknowledge the stress your body underwent and be compassionate towards yourself.

If your varicose veins are severe or painful, you might want to consider surgery to remove them. However, this is rarely needed. Consult with your GP if you have any continued discomfort.

Postpartum Hair Loss

Many women deal with postpartum hair loss. It is not something you should worry about, and no, you will not go bald. It merely means your body needs a while longer to get back to its usual self. By the time your baby is one, your hair loss will slow down, and your mane will go back to its pre-pregnancy glory. The simplest way to ensure your hair's health is to take prenatal vitamin supplements even after pregnancy. Don't expose your hair to any heat or chemical treatments. Take extra care while washing your hair after pregnancy. Consider using headscarves to protect your hair from damage by the weather or using scrunchies instead of rubber bands. If you notice excessive hair loss, seek medical help and contact your GP.

How to Recover Faster from a C-Section

If you underwent a C-section, then your recovery will take longer than natural birth. Even though it's a little harder on your body, don't fret; you can use some tips to speed up the recovery process.

For example, hug a pillow snugly against the C-section incision, whenever you cough or sneeze, to splint the incision and stitches. It not only reduces the pain but eases the pressure on the incision too. A common side effect of any form of abdominal surgery is constipation. Make it a point to consume a high fibre diet and take a stool softener, as directed by your midwife, doctor or health visitor.

If your midwife or doctor prescribes any pain medications, you can take them even while breastfeeding. Ensure that you take them as directed to reduce any discomfort.

Avoid lifting any weights heavier than your baby, and get as much rest as you possibly can. If you've heard any myths about breastfeeding after a caesarean, remember it is purely a myth. Irrespective of whether it was a vaginal birth or a C-section, both mothers can successfully breastfeed their newborns. While breastfeeding your baby, try to position them away from the incision to avoid any discomfort. Until the doctor or the midwife removes the stitches over the incision at the postpartum check, they will stay in place. If you notice any soreness, redness, or the incision opens and bleeds, or if there is any greenish-yellow discharge from the incision, seek medical help immediately.

Take extra care of your body while it's healing. An essential aspect of recovery is your diet, which should be nutritious and well-balanced. Your diet is even more important if you are breastfeeding. Drink plenty of fluids to stay hydrated.

If you have any doubts, never hesitate to call your GP or midwife immediately. It is quite common for new mothers to fear their safety and their child's well-being. You are not paranoid, and don't let anyone else tell you otherwise. If something troubles or bothers you, seek help immediately.

All these tips are quite simple. If you are a little patient, compassionate, and careful, recovery becomes relatively easy.

2

WHAT SHOULD I EAT?

As I talk to expectant and new mothers from around the globe, I hear many of the same questions. For example: "What should I feed my baby?" "Is breast milk sufficient?" "Should I consider formula?" "Which one is better, and why? What should I eat?" "Why is it important for me to maintain a healthy diet?"

D o these questions sound familiar to you? If yes, you aren't alone. All mums have these concerns. You will learn the answers to all these questions in this chapter.

It is not only essential to ensure that your baby gets the nourishment he needs, but your health matters, too. Postpartum nutrition is incredibly vital for your overall health and recovery. You might have some doubts about how and what to feed the baby. Likewise, you might be worried about your nutritional needs too. Don't worry because, in this chapter, I will introduce you to some simple tips you can use to ensure that you and your baby get the ideal nourishment.

Your Baby

When it comes to feeding your baby, there are two options. You can either bottle-feed or breastfeed. Bottle-feeding is an effective alternative to breastfeeding. Several new mums who cannot breastfeed their baby, or wish to use baby formula while occasionally breastfeeding their baby, usually opt for bottle-feeding. You also have the option to feed breast milk to your little one through bottles.

One of the first acts of nurturing your little one as a new mother is breastfeeding. Breastfeeding is quite natural, but plenty of women worry and stress about it. As long as you consume a healthy diet and take care of yourself, your breast milk has all the nutrients your baby needs. If you wish to breastfeed your baby, you should be aware of a couple of things.

Breastfeeding has many advantages for your baby and for you, the mother, too. According to NHS England and the World Health Organisation, it is recommended to give nothing but breast milk to your child for the first 26 weeks – 6 months. This is because breast milk can protect your little one against any viruses, infections, and is easy to digest filled with nutrients and vitamins your baby needs. Breast-milk can also reduce the risk of the sudden infant death syndrome (SIDS), obesity and cardiovascular disease in adulthood.

Since breastmilk is free and naturally made by your body for your little one, you save some money by not buying formula as a new mother. Apart from that stunning discovery, you have a lowered risk of breast cancer, osteoporosis (weak bones), obesity, ovarian cancer, and cardiovascular disease when you breastfeed.

Now that we have covered the benefits let's talk about the struggles new mothers face whilst breastfeeding their little one.

Tongue-tie

Tongue-tie is when the strip of skin connecting the baby's tongue to the bottom of their mouth is shorter than average. If your baby has tongue-tie, it can restrict the tongues movement leading to other breastfeeding problems like improper latching on to the breast, sore nipples and mastitis.

Symptoms of tongue-tie are:

- Your baby may feed for a long time, but still, seem unsatisfied and almost unsettled
- Your baby's tongue does not lift or move side to side
- Your baby may not gain weight as quickly as he or she should

If you suspect your baby may have tongue-tie or are just concerned about it, always contact your GP or health visitor and discuss this concern with them.

Sore Nipples

One of the leading causes of sore nipples is when your baby does not latch properly at the breast. This is pretty common as a newbie breastfeeder and especially in the first few weeks of breastfeeding. With sore nipples, you may experience cracked or sensitive nipples too. If, however, you have nipple pain at every feeding and your nipples start to bleed, immediately get in contact with your midwife, health visitor or breastfeeding specialist. This is because cracked and/or bleeding nipples have more of an increased chance of catching an infection.

I'd also suggest you ask your midwife, health visitor or breastfeeding specialist for help with how to position your baby to latch correctly on to your breast. This is because they would usually watch you feed your baby and actively help position your baby correctly to latch on.

When I had sore nipples, I would try to shorten my breast-feeding sessions to sort of ease my pain but DO NOT do this. I told my midwife what I was doing, and she pointed out that breast milk works on a supply and demand system, so the less I feed, the less I produce. But for me, the pain was really unbearable, so she recommended that I try a hand expressing method – honestly, this was like stumbling on gold. Suppose you want to learn more about what the hand expressing method is. In that case, a quick YouTube search can provide you with some helpful and informative videos, which are usually created by mothers, midwives and health professionals.

Here are some home treatment techniques for sore nipples:

- Consider switching to cotton bras, as they help air to circulate better around the nipples for the nipples to airdry faster and minimises the chance for irritation between the nipples and any clothing

- Continue to breastfeed as shortening your feeding sessions will not ease the pain and can be counterproductive - the National Institute for Health Care and Excellence (NICE) 'Advise the woman to continue breastfeeding wherever possible and advise that reducing the duration of feeds is unlikely to relieve nipple pain'
- For pain, you can try some cold compress or ice packs after and/or between feeding sessions
- If you experience cracked nipples, dabbing some expressed milk on the breast and nipples can promote healing as breast milk contains natural skin softeners and also antibodies that can fight off infections whilst your nipples heal

Thrush

Thrush is a fungal infection in the breasts. Breastfed babies can also develop thrush in their mouths, but don't fret as thrush is easily treatable. The fungus, candida, can enter your breast or nipple when your nipples are sore or cracked, which can be caused when your baby does not latch on at the breast properly.

Thrush can be a reason for feeling nipple and breast pain, but so can sore nipples too (the result of improper positioning of your baby to latch on) and vice versa. This is why it is essential to contact your midwife, GP, or professional health visitor because they have the equipment and experience to differentiate between them and give you the right solution and treatment.

The perfect environment for the fungus - candida - to

develop has to be warm and moist; breastfeeding creates that.

The symptoms of thrush infections to look out for in breastfeeding women are:

- A sudden start of pain in BOTH breasts and/or nipples after breastfeeding having formerly not experienced any pain after breastfeeding
- The pain is severe, burning and sharp; this pain lasts up to 1 hour after breastfeeding

The symptoms of thrush infections in breastfed babies are:

- Creamy white patches in your baby's mouth, gums, on the tongue and further back or inside of the cheeks – please note that the creamy white patches won't rub off
- Your baby's tongue or lips may have a white gloss
- Your baby feeling unsettled during and between feedings

If you think you and/or your child may have thrush, please call your GP or health visitor. They will arrange for swabs to be taken from your nipple and your baby's mouth to confirm this and give you and your baby the appropriate treatment. They may prescribe antifungal cream or tablets for you, the mum, and cream or gel to give to your baby. Your doctor/nurse will tell you exactly how to use the treatment, so don't worry about that.

Mastitis

Mastitis is when your breasts become inflamed, swollen and feel painful. Mastitis is caused by a build-up of milk in the milk ducts, so the breasts produce more milk than is being removed. A build-up of milk can be caused by:

1. Your baby not latching on to your breast properly
2. Your milk ducts are damaged through some sort of injury
3. You're using one breast more than the other one for breastfeeding

Here are some quick tips for home treatment:

- Keep breastfeeding and aim for at least 8-12 feeds a day as this can increase how much milk is being removed and reduce the build-up of milk in the milk ducts
- Placing a warm cloth on your breasts may relieve some pain
- You can also use gel pads for your breasts that have cooling or warming effects to reduce and alleviate the pain
- Paracetamol and ibuprofen can be used to also relieve the pain and avoid aspirin at all costs – please consult with your midwife or GP before taking these medicines just so you're sure you can take it; every mother is indeed different
- Hand express milk from your breasts in between feedings and store the excess the milk
- Rest and drink fluids regularly

- Massage the area around your breasts and move to your nipples (repeat action back and forth) to clear any blockages

If after 2-3 days you still feel these home treatment tips have not worked, please get in touch with your GP or health visitor and explain to them that your breasts are swollen, inflamed and/or feel painful. They may likely prescribe you some medicine, ask you to come in for an examination or refer you to a midwife or breastfeeding specialist.

Leaking

During the first few weeks of breastfeeding, your breasts might "leak." It is natural. It usually happens when you hear a baby cry. Leaking can also occur if the baby hasn't been fed for a couple of hours, when you think about the baby, or experience any strong emotions. It's a psychological reaction, which triggers the production of milk. As your baby continues to nurse, the leaking will also stop. Once again, this shows how your body is intrinsically hardwired to take care of your offspring.

Engorgement

Engorgement happens when your breasts produce more milk than your baby consumes. It causes swelling and hardening of the breasts and can be quite uncomfortable. Engorgement usually occurs when your first milk comes after the baby is delivered. The swelling can make it tricky to feed your baby.

If the engorgement persists, gently massage the areola

between your fingers. It usually goes away after feeding your baby. An ice pack or cold compress can help relieve any pains and reduce the swelling. A warm shower also helps the milk flow smoothly. Additionally, you can use a breast pump and continue to pump out the excess milk until the breast is soft and feels normal.

Stress

A common reason for stress for new mothers is worrying that their body will not produce sufficient milk. All mammals are biologically programmed to produce sufficient milk to take care of their young ones. Milk production often depends on the needs of your baby. Whenever your baby sucks your breasts, it stimulates the production of oxytocin and prolactin, further stimulating the production of milk. The more frequently your baby nurses, the more milk your body produces.

If you notice any yellowish-orange fluid oozing from your breasts during the first couple of days, don't worry. This is known as colostrum; it is incredibly nutritious and contains high amounts of antibodies that your baby needs. As mentioned, your body knows what to do, even if you think you don't. So, rest easy because things have a way of working themselves out.

Baby's Cue

Some mothers may struggle to know when their baby needs to be fed. So, instead of waiting for your baby to start crying, there are some simple cues you can look out for to anticipate his hunger. He might raise or turn his head repeatedly, open and close his mouth; suck on whatever is near him, or even stick his tongue out. If you notice he is making these moves, it means it's time for a feeding.

Time Limit

There is no fixed time limit for a feeding session. As soon as your baby is full, she will let go of your nipple and stop sucking. Once she is full, her head might tilt back, and she will seem drowsy. This is also a sign that breastfeeding is going on well. Don't try to establish a specific schedule when nursing your infant right away. Also, don't wake up and feed a sleeping baby, merely because it's been three hours since her last feeding. Allow your baby to determine the routine and stick to it.

When to Seek Support

Reading about breastfeeding and taking classes is quite different from actually doing it. Within the first hour of your child's birth, you'll be asked to breastfeed him. Usually, the doctors, nurse, or midwife shows you how to do it. If you need some extra help, don't hesitate to ask for it immediately. There is no shame in not knowing what to do. You are a new mother; cut yourself some slack.

Low Breast Milk Supply?

There are different foods you can eat to increase your breast milk supply. This will ensure your little one is always well-fed. Here are some foods I consciously added to my diet when I nursed my babies.

Seeds

Carom seeds
Fenugreek seeds
Cumin seeds
Poppy seeds
Anise seeds
Sesame seeds
Chia seeds

Grains, Legumes, and Dairy Products

Barley
Oatmeal
Brown rice
Chickpeas
Cow's milk
Healthy fats (peanut oil, olive oil, clarified butter, and coconut oil)
Yoghurt
All types of legumes

Vegetables

Carrots
Spinach
Sweet potato
Ginger
Garlic
Moringa leaves
Bottle gourd
Green papaya

Asparagus
Bitter gourd

Herbs

Alfalfa
Shatavari
Turmeric
Dill leaves
Blessed thistle
Basil

Other Options

Eggs
Seafood and lean meats
Almonds and all types of nuts
Water and fruit juices
Milk tea
Brewer's yeast
Apricots

Bottle-feeding and Formula

I know a few mothers prefer formula or can't breastfeed for various acceptable reasons. Below are advantages of using a formula and bottle-feeding to show that it is okay to use formula and not feel like your 'less' of a mother. Every mother is different, BUT you're still a mother, and you should be proud of that fact.

Benefits of Bottle Feeding and Formula

Anyone Can Do It

Perhaps the most vital benefit of bottle feeding or using a formula is that anyone can feed your baby. With breast-feeding, you're the only one that can do this for them. However, you can equally divide all responsibilities with your partner, loved ones or other caregivers in your baby's life using a formula and bottle-feeding. Also, it becomes easier to feed your baby in public, and you may feel more comfortable.

Keep Track of Baby's Intake

All new moms are required to track their baby's intake of milk. It can be overwhelming and hectic during the first couple of weeks that you lose track of all this. When you use a bottle, you know how much your baby is consuming. It becomes easier to keep track of their intake. For example, there were instances when I had no idea how much my little one was eating, and if it was sufficient. With formula and/or bottle-feeding, you will always know how much they are eating and how much they're supposed to be fed. This is not always necessary, but it certainly offers peace of mind.

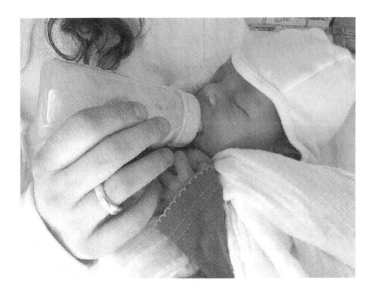

Use Medication

After a C-section, you might be on several pain medications to ease the surgery's painful after-effects. These painkillers might adversely affect the quality and supply of your breast milk. In such instances, it is better to use a formula. Most of the painkillers prescribed to new moms after surgery are often safe, even while breastfeeding. However, the worry doesn't go away. Taking care of a new baby can be a little scary and overwhelming. So, it is naturally stressful for you. Worrying about the effect of medication on your breast milk merely increases the stress you experience.

Change Your Diet

You can have coffee or a glass of wine without worrying if you use formula. Yes, I know it sounds a little selfish, but it is a viable reason. You can eat spicy food, take pain medication, or use any other medicines you want for your health conditions without any worries. It can also help you regain your sense of self after having a baby when you can do all these things. Pregnancy comes with a variety of restrictions you need to follow for the well-being of your baby. Once it comes to an end, you should concentrate on yourself. If you are not in the best of moods, it will affect your little one. Therefore, it is crucial to prioritise not just your baby's health, but also your well-being. Your sense of self might be an intangible complement of your mental health, but it is incredibly important.

Time Management

Bottle-feeding reduces the time spent on your baby's feeding sessions. All you need to do is merely make the formula, store it in a bottle, and it's ready to use. You can pump your breast milk and keep it ready for your little one, but this isn't always easy. By using the formula, all the time you save can be used for other activities. You can spend more time with your little one or take care of any other obligations you have without any worries. As a new mom, you will need all the rest you can get. Bottle-feeding helps achieve this simple objective.

Lactose Intolerance

There are cases when the infant can be lactose intolerant. Such infants cannot process animal milk or breast milk. In such cases, using formula may be the best option available. Suitable baby formula for lactose-intolerant infants is made of soy protein and directly fed from a bottle.

Mother's Health Condition

There are instances when mothers are not in their best physical health after childbirth. If the mother falls ill after the delivery or faces any health complications, breast-feeding is not viable. If the mother decides to breastfeed, it not only compromises her health but isn't good for her

Newborn either. To maintain the mother and her baby's health, bottle-feeding may be a good idea.

Mother's Mental Health

Most of us talk about physical health but forget that mental health is equally important, even more so for a new mother. Your body just underwent a significant transition, and welcoming a new baby into your life can be stressful. Yes, you will be thrilled, but the stress is real. We often talk about doing the best for the baby. However, it is equally important that you are happy as well. If you are happy, your baby will be happy. Never let anyone devalue your physical, mental, emotional well-being.

Breastfeeding is helpful, but using formula isn't a bad thing. With bottle feeding, you can rest easy knowing your baby is getting all the nourishment he needs. This reduces a lot of stress of being a new mother. It, in turn, will make you feel better, which will make your baby feel better.

What to Eat for Yourself

Food List when Breastfeeding

While breastfeeding your little one, try to include the previous section's food items in your meals. As long as you consume a healthy and well-balanced diet, you have nothing to be worried about. Try to include starchy foods, whole grains, and plenty of vegetables. You can also add some dairy products such as milk, yoghurt, and clarified butter. Add some lean meats and seafood to ensure your body gets its share of protein and healthy fats.

You might need to eat more frequently than usual, to

produce sufficient milk to support your little one. You can consume seafood but try to limit it to no more than once or twice a week. Drink plenty of water and electrolytes to keep yourself thoroughly hydrated. If you feel fatigued or your pee is dark yellow and has a strong smell, it's a sign of dehydration. You don't need any extra calories while breastfeeding, but ensure that you consume a healthy diet. Avoid caffeinated drinks, alcohol, and unhealthy junk food during this period. These unhealthy foods can pass on from your body to your baby via breast milk.

Food List if Using Formula

If your baby is using a formula, you can make any changes to your diet as required. Don't start with any restrictive diets immediately after delivery. Give your body a couple of weeks to recover, and then you can concentrate on losing the pregnancy weight. An unhealthy diet will harm the recovery process and increase the strain on your body. Try to snack frequently and eat small meals instead of three big meals. Include plenty of healthy green vegetables and low-carb vegetables to your diet.

You can occasionally consume coffee and drink alcohol if you want because your baby is consuming the formula. However, try to limit the intake of such foods until you have recovered fully. Also, if you're trying to lose weight, then avoid all these things. Drink plenty of fluids, herbal teas, and avoid unhealthy junk food. Before you opt to go on a diet, ensure that you talk to your GP.

3

DON'T MAKE SLEEP A PRIVILEGE

*My baby is such a blessing, and we're so happy to have
him in our lives. Of course, since we've come home from
the hospital, we're not getting much sleep. Even the dog
has been "complaining!" I know that we can't expect our
newborn to sleep through the night until he's a little older.
But what are some things that we can do to make sure we
all get the sleep we need? We'd like to have more children,
and we know that learning for our first baby will be better
for everyone in the future. Thanks for your help!"*

- Allison

I have been asked a lot of questions from new mothers.
However, there is one question that comes up all the
time. "My baby has a hard time sleeping through the
night... I have tried... Do you have any tips for how to help
my baby (and me!) sleep?"

Many new moms (and dads) struggle to get just a few hours of sleep at night. After all, how can they sleep when every moment of their life is dedicated to taking care of their new baby?

Well, you shouldn't make sleep a privilege. I remember all the sleepless nights I had after the birth of my first child. I was running on fumes, and it was anything but easy. It made me tired, anxious, frustrated, and exhausted. It took a toll on my mental health. I don't want this to happen to you, so you should start prioritising sleep.

Do you remember the wonderful nightly activity you used to partake in daily? When you would lie down on a comfortable bed and sleep soundly for 8 hours or so? Oh well, if you are a new parent, this would seem like a distant dream or a thing of the past. Welcoming a baby into your home and life is not just pleasant but is downright ecstatic. I felt this too! However, there is one thing no one prepares you for, and that's all the sleepless nights that come with this. A majority of new parents hardly get any good quality of sleep.

Most of us believe that sleep is a single state of unconsciousness. However, there are two types of sleep: rapid eye movement (REM) or dream sleep and non-REM. Non-REM consists of four stages. In the first stage, you start to feel drowsy while your body relaxes. In the second stage, your body and eye movements stop while your brainwaves slow down. In the third and the fourth stages, you are in deep sleep where your breathing is regular, and you don't respond to anything around you. An adult goes through these four stages in 90 minutes and repeats them around 4 to 6 times while sleeping at night.

Your baby's sleep patterns are nothing like this. Until he is three months old, about 50 to 80% of his sleep will be REM, while yours is only 20%. Also, his sleep cycles are completed within 15 minutes, while yours take 90 minutes. It is vital to understand these things because your baby will spend most of his time sleeping while you are taking care of him. Are you wondering why it would be difficult if a baby sleeps all the time? Babies not only fall asleep quickly, but they wake up from their sleep also quite fast. He will sleep, but it will only be for short periods, usually no longer than 2-4 hours.

Getting sufficient sleep is quintessential for your well-being. Not just your physical health, but your mental health too. If your body doesn't get the rest it needs, it cannot function effectively. After all, it needs all the rest it can get to recover from childbirth. However, there is one common mistake many new parents make; they start treating sleep as a luxury.

No, sleep is a basic need, and you should account for it. You can use simple tips to get better sleep at night and help your baby sleep through the night. This might not be possible in the initial weeks, but you can start doing this after a while. This section will show you how you can help your baby sleep better through the night and improve your sleep as a first-time mum.

Healthy Sleeping Habits for Your Baby

Babies aren't accustomed to the concept of day and night. They will take a while to get used to a regular sleeping schedule. Their tummies are quite small and get full rather quickly. So, they need to be fed at regular intervals, which is another reason they need night feedings. As your baby grows, her body will develop, and the number of night feedings she needs will also reduce. Until then, let's look at straightforward ideas you can use to create a bedtime routine for your little one. The sooner you start using these ideas, the easier it will be to get her habituated to a specific routine.

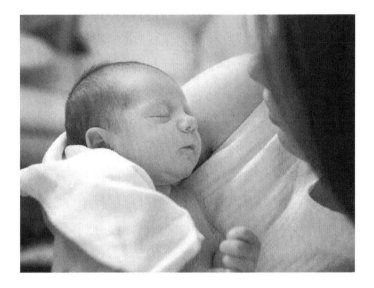

The first step to create a healthy sleeping routine for your baby is to teach her the difference between daytime and night-time. During the day, have some fun, spend time together, play games with her, and don't worry about any daily noise when she naps. At night, ensure that the lights are always dim, there isn't much noise, and you put your baby down to sleep as soon as she had been fed and changed. Unless your baby needs it, don't feed her and don't play with her at night. After a while, your baby will understand the difference between day and night.

Until your baby is six months old, ensure that he sleeps in the same room as you, not necessarily on the same bed, but in the same room. During the first couple of weeks, you might notice your baby falls asleep only when you are holding him, or someone else is. As soon as your baby has had his feed or has fallen asleep in your arms, slowly put him down to sleep without any sleeping crutches.

Newborns usually sleep frequently throughout the day and night. However, you have the liberty to change your schedule so that it is comfortable for you too. For instance, here's a small trick I learned along the way. Instead of worrying about night-time feeds, I always used to feed my baby before going to sleep. This helped me sleep for a while longer at night.

Establish a simple bedtime routine that enables your baby to sleep at night. You can introduce this as soon as your baby is about three months old. A simple and soothing bedtime routine helps not just the baby, but also you, and prevents the chances of any sleeping troubles later. Having a bath, changing your baby's clothes, putting him to bed, and reading a simple bedtime story can be a part of his bedtime routine. You can also dim the lights, give him a good night kiss and cuddle, sing a lullaby, play some soothing music, or brush his teeth (if he has any) as part of the bedtime routine.

All these simple patterns will soon become a part of his bedtime routine. Ensure that there is a little time between your baby's last feed and bedtime. If you feed your baby to sleep, he will soon start getting used to the idea that he needs to sleep only after receiving a feed. Therefore, give a little break between these two activities. Newborns usually sleep between 8-16 and 18 hours daily. So, having a bedtime routine is quite pivotal.

Two Methods to Get Your Newborn to Sleep

1. Laugh Together

One of the main reasons why a baby refuses to sleep is because of the anxiety she feels. Tension might be why your child doesn't sleep. In such situations, the most powerful ally you can count on is laughter. Therefore, laugh together with your little one, and she will feel safe. It also alleviates any stress she experiences. Even if it sounds like a weird idea, it works effectively.

When you look at things from your baby's perspective, you will realise that the world is quite scary. She is not used to their world, yet, and it will take some time to get comfortable. This is a common reason why babies experience a little anxiety and tension. If she keeps waking up or starts crying while sleeping, she might be anxious about something. You can tickle your baby and make her smile or laugh a little before bedtime. If you can help alleviate your baby's anxiety, it improves her chances of sleeping through the night.

2. Soothing Music

It is always suggested that you need to create a quiet environment for your baby to sleep at night. However, I found another technique that seems to work wonderfully well. Instead of trying to create a quiet environment, you can play some soothing music. Soothing music or soft lullabies help relieve the anxiety your newborn feels and make him feel safe. Another alternative to playing music is using white noise. You can use a white noise machine or even play some white noise music from YouTube videos. These techniques work brilliantly well, and they are quite simple.

Ways to Improve Sleep for First-Time Mothers

Life seldom turns out the way you expect. This stands true for motherhood too. Now that the baby is here, it might not be like you hoped it would. Of course, you love your baby more than you ever imagined you could love anyone. But it might be weeks, or even months before you get a good night's sleep. All the time, you have is now dedicated to taking care of the needs of your newborn.

It isn't easy to take care of your needs or your baby when you are sleep deprived. Sleep deprivation can harm the quality of your life and your overall health. From drowsy driving to an increase in the risk of postpartum mental health problems, sleep deprivation is clearly undesirable. It might seem impossible to sleep through the night when you have a crying infant. However, I believe some simple tips will come in handy and help improve your sleep as a first-time mom.

Outsource Tasks

Learn to outsource responsibilities when you have an infant to take care of. You might be tempted to do everything by yourself, but it just isn't physically possible. Even if you manage to do this for a week or two, the tiredness will soon catch up. If there is any task that can be performed by anyone else, delegate it immediately. Once you outsource the task, don't worry about it. For instance, if you decide to bottle-feed your baby, ask your partner or anyone in the household to do this. Divide all the household responsibilities as much as you can to take some time for yourself.

Say Yes to Help

You might not want to accept it, but you will need all the help you can get like we just mentioned. So, when help comes your way, take it. Learn to say yes to help. Let go of any preconceived notions you have about being a multi-tasker. All this can wait until your baby grows up. The only priority is to ensure that you get sufficient sleep and rest your body needs to recover. Whether by a friend, family member, or a babysitter, accept their help so you can catch up on a couple of hours of sleep or some free time outside of the house.

Sleep When Your Baby Sleeps

A simple tip I received after my first pregnancy was to sleep whenever my baby slept. This is the simplest way to keep postpartum sleep deprivation at bay. Whenever your baby naps, forget about all the other tasks you need to complete and, instead, catch up on some much-needed sleep.

Many new mothers make a common mistake because they are tempted to do many other things when their babies sleep. Perhaps you want to do the dishes, clean the house, catch up on some work, or even talk to your loved ones. However, all these things can wait, but your sleep cannot. Moreover, if you manage to get just six hours of sleep each day, it helps avoid sleep deprivation. Learn to accept that all these things are part of becoming a new mother and don't try to be a perfectionist. Once your baby is up, even you need to be. It doesn't matter if there is a laundry lying around the house, but if you are too tired to drive your baby to his doctor's appointment, you have a real problem on hand. Start prioritising sleep, and don't treat it as a luxury.

The 'Don'ts' of Fatigue and Tiredness

Multiple feedings, unexpected nappy changes at odd hours, and a lot of fuzziness can turn anyone into a sleep-deprived zombie. Here is some advice you should follow to avoid fatigue and tiredness.

Remember the Importance of Exercise and Diet

There is a bidirectional relationship between exercise and sleep and diet and sleep. If you consume healthy and well-balanced meals, it improves your quality of sleep at night. When you sleep at night and get the rest you need, it becomes easier to stick to a healthy diet. Likewise, when you exercise, it improves your quality of sleep at night. When you get sufficient rest at night, it makes you feel more energetic.

Therefore, start to prioritise healthy eating habits, include some form of physical activity whenever you can to stay energetic during the day, and get better sleep at night.

Don't Drink Coffee Before Sleeping

When you are sleep deprived, it can be quite tempting to reach out for an additional cup of coffee. The instant boost of caffeine might make you feel energetic, but it will eventually tire you out. Also, you cannot consume any caffeine if you are breastfeeding your little one. Don't start using caffeine as a crutch to stay awake. If you keep drinking coffee at odd hours to stay awake, sleeping at night will become even more difficult.

Don't Ignore the Power of a Nap

A good nap can make you feel instantly energetic and reduce sleep deprivation. Never disregard the importance of a catnap. Although naps cannot substitute the overall effect of eight hours of quality sleep, they certainly help in the long run. Even if you sleep for about 20 minutes, you will feel better, be more alert, and feel instantly energetic. This energy boost is critical while taking care of your newborn.

I highly recommend you set your nap alarm for about thirty minutes. If you sleep longer than that, it can have the reverse effect, and you might become drowsy. This happens because that longer time allows you to go into a deeper sleep, which is hard to interrupt. When you wake up, you tend to be more tired instead of refreshed, as you would be with a shorter nap.

Don't Make Sleeping Pills Your Friend

Resist the temptation of popping sleep meds to get better sleep. Even if you have the time to nap, but don't feel like it, force yourself to sleep instead of using any sleep medication. Don't use any sleep medication, especially without the approval of your doctor. The right pill might be an occasional sleeping aid, but try to avoid it as much as possible. If you want to regulate your sleep cycle, try to use the previous section's tips to improve your sleep quality at night.

Don't Disregard Sleep Deprivation Signs

Whenever you are sleep deprived, your body will tell

you. If you notice any of these symptoms, the only solution is to get sufficient sleep. A lack of sleep can harm your cognition and physical performance to the point that you might seem and feel like you are going insane. The prolonged effect of sleep deprivation can result in obesity, diabetes, hypertension, depression, anxiety, cardiovascular diseases, and even impairing your glucose tolerance. Suppose you experience mood swings, blurred vision, and fluctuations in your appetite, or have trouble concentrating. In that case, these are all signs of sleep deprivation. Pay close attention to how your body feels.

General Tips to Feel More Energetic

You can make a couple of simple changes to your daily schedule and your baby's sleep schedule to feel energised. As a new mama, there is one important fact you need to make peace with; that is, you will no longer get uninterrupted sleep at night. Taking care of all your baby's needs will be your priority, but it will tire you out as well. In this section, let's look at easy pointers you can use to feel more energetic.

Let Go of Your Expectations

Do not hold on to any expectations. The more you try to control things, the more drained you will feel. Accept the simple truth that things will be different, and instead of fighting this change, accept it. As soon as you wake up in the morning, tell yourself you will approach the day with a positive mindset and attitude. Don't try to swim against the tide and, instead, go with the flow, and you will feel better. Irrespective of whether it's an all-day screaming fest or your baby's first giggle, you cannot predict how life turns out.

Learn to embrace every day as a new beginning. And you will feel better about yourself.

Eat Well

Again, pay close attention to the diet you consume. Every meal or snack you consume should be rich in protein and digestive fibre. These foods not only make you feel energetic but also leave you feeling full for longer. If you are in a rush to lose all the baby weight, then paying attention to your diet can do wonders in the long run. Don't binge on any unhealthy snacks. Once you start paying attention to the food you consume, it will immediately improve your overall mood and sense of well-being.

Regular and Moderate Exercise

Do not get used to a sedentary lifestyle. Instead, try to include some form of physical activity. It's necessary to do this, even if it is just walking around the house for 20 minutes daily. You can see the benefits of daily exercise within a few weeks. It comes in handy, especially if you're trying to lose all the baby weight you gained during pregnancy. As mentioned in the previous section, exercise also helps you sleep better at night. Once you start taking good care of yourself, your overall mood and attitude towards life also improve.

'Me Time'

I know, having a baby is a full-time activity. You might not have any time left for yourself at the end of the day. However, irrespective of how tiring or hectic your daily schedule is, take some time out for yourself. Even if it is as little as 20 minutes, it will make you feel better. In these 20 minutes, do something you genuinely enjoy and love. Perhaps you can read a book, watch a movie, or even just sit by yourself. Take a long, relaxing bath if you want or meditate and silence. This me-time is vital for your emotional and mental well-being.

<u>Go Outside</u>

You can sit in the front yard with your little one, take a walk around the block, or visit a local park. Spend a short time outdoors, and it will instantly energise you. Being out in the sunshine not only makes you happy but increases the production of serotonin. Serotonin is a chemical that instantly elevates your mood. It ensures that you get your daily vitamin D dose, which is extremely important for your cognitive function, immune system, and bone health. Also, when you get a break from your usual surroundings, you will feel better.

4

YOUR MENTAL HEALTH IS JUST AS IMPORTANT!

I love my baby so much, and my husband has been incredibly supportive. Friends come by and visit, and things 'should' be great. But I have an overwhelming sadness that I can't seem to shake. At first, I thought it was because there were so many changes in our lives, but it's been a few months now. I cry at the drop of a hat, for no reason at all, and I think I might be depressed. I don't want to tell my partner because I don't want him to worry. He's so happy and proud of our new family. What should I do?

- Jennifer

New mothers often ask me, "Is it normal to experience a roller coaster of emotions? One minute I am smiling, and the next, I am anxious." Well, if you feel like this, it is okay. Welcoming a baby into your life is not just a physical change but also a mental and emotional one. My advice is that you stop worrying about it and make time for a little self-care. Taking care of your diet, for example, helps your body and provides a little TLC for your mental health.

Welcoming a baby into your life is not just a significant milestone in your life, but it is also a huge lifestyle change. From your everyday activities to your sleep schedule and priorities, everything changes when your little one comes home. At times, moms can feel a little overwhelmed because of all these changes. Unless you learn to deal with these changes, chances are you will be caught off-guard. Change is often scary, and it can take a toll on your mental and emotional well-being if you aren't careful.

New mothers tend to feel emotional, stressed, and frustrated at times. All this is understandable because you are trying to cope with all the new responsibilities and demands of motherhood while also getting through your daily routine and life. Your sleep schedule changes, there will be fluctuations in your appetite, and you'll probably experience several mood swings and more stress.

All these things are not only common, but you should expect them too. Many people concentrate on their physical well-being, but they fail to pay the same attention to their mental health. Your mental health is as important as your physical health. If you don't take care of this, it will take a toll on your quality of life and get in the way of all the happiness and joys associated with motherhood. In this section, let's look at some of the common mental health concerns a new mum might experience.

Postpartum Anxiety

What Is It?

All new moms tend to worry about their little ones, and it is natural to do this. You might wonder if he is eating well, getting sufficient sleep, or hitting all the right milestones. You might also be worried about your lack of sleep, all the chores you need to complete, or something else. It is not just normal, but it is also a healthy sign of all the love you have for your baby. However, if this anxiety doesn't go away, regardless of what you do, or if you feel on edge all the time because of it, or it keeps you up at night, it might be more than "jitters." One common health condition many people are aware of is postpartum depression. Well, it turns out, postpartum anxiety is also common.

What are the Common Symptoms?

All new parents experience some anxiety and worry to a certain extent. If left unchecked, it can quickly overwhelm you and evolve into postpartum anxiety.

Common symptoms of postpartum anxiety include:

- You experience constant worry and fear, which cannot be eased.
- The feeling of dread about something going wrong.
- Sleep disruption.
- An inability to control your racing mind.

Sleep disruption is frequent for all new parents, but if you find yourself staying up at wee hours of the night because you cannot sleep, or are experiencing troubling thoughts that don't go away, you may be dealing with an anxiety disorder.

The different symptoms of postpartum anxiety disorder

can also manifest themselves as physical symptoms. The most common physical signs of postpartum anxiety disorder include:

- Nausea
- Vomiting
- Fatigue
- Hyperventilation
- Heart palpitations
- Shakiness and trembling
- Sweating

If you notice any or all the symptoms discussed in this section, seek medical help immediately. It is something you shouldn't worry about; openly discuss your concerns with your midwife, health visitor or GP.

What are the Probable Causes?

It is quite reasonable to feel anxious, especially if you are a first-time mother. When every product you purchase comes with a warning in caps about SIDS (sudden infant death syndrome), it increases your worry. All the ricocheting hormones in your body could be the reason for postpartum anxiety disorder. Hormone fluctuations are universal, but only some suffer from a postpartum anxiety disorder, while others don't. Therefore, it is still a bit of a mystery. However, some factors increase your risk of this disorder. Any history of eating disorders, intense mood-related symptoms synced with your menstrual cycle, or any previous pregnancy-related traumatic episodes such as a miscarriage or the loss of a baby, can trigger postpartum anxiety disorder.

Possible Treatment

The first step to treat postpartum anxiety disorder is to

get diagnosed. Don't stay silent about any symptoms you notice and ensure that you don't miss any postpartum checkups with the doctor. The first checkup is usually within the first six weeks of the delivery, and it is something you should attend without any fail. Postpartum anxiety disorder not only affects your mental and physical well-being, but it also harms the bond you share with your baby. Start discussing any symptoms you notice with your doctor, take the prescribed medications, recommended supplements, and complementary treatments, or talk to a mental health specialist. The different activities you can perform can help ease anxiety, such as relaxation techniques, mindfulness, and physical exercise.

Postpartum Depression

What Is It?

You might have come across the term "baby blues." It is often described as a condition wherein new mothers tend to feel fatigued, sad, or worried, for no apparent reason. Most mothers experience all these feelings within a week or two after the delivery. However, this is normal, and it usually goes away with time. The terms postpartum depression and "baby blues" might sound the same, but they are not. Postpartum depression is not only more potent, but it also lasts for longer.

From severe mood swings to a sense of utter hopelessness and exhaustion, there are different problems associated with this condition. It isn't something that needs to be taken lightly and should be treated immediately. There is no shame in talking about your mental health, and it is crucial for your overall well-being and the bond you share with your child.

What are the Common Symptoms?

After childbirth, it is natural to feel tired, irritable, or even moody for some time. However, postpartum depression is so much more than this, and it can effectively prevent you from functioning normally. The common symptoms of postpartum depression are exhaustion, and an inability to sleep. Perhaps you sleep too much, feel sad or cry excessively for no apparent reason (even if things are going well). You might experience unexplainable aches, pains, or illnesses that cannot be adequately diagnosed. Either you lose your appetite completely, or binge eat. You often feel out of control and have trouble recollecting things. You cannot make simple decisions; you have a tough time concentrating on the task at hand and feel irritable, anxious, and angry for no reason. You may lose interest in things that you used to enjoy, feel overwhelming grief and hopelessness.

With postpartum depression, you might be overcome with feelings of worthlessness and guilt about the feelings you have. You often feel disconnected from your baby and wonder why you're not experiencing happiness, as everyone told you, you would. You feel yourself withdrawing from everyone and everything in general. Another common symptom is that you start experiencing intrusive thoughts about self-harm or harming the baby.

I know all this can sound terrifying. However, it is a mental health problem, and it needs to be addressed immediately. The sooner you seek help, the better it is for your well-being.

What are the Probable Causes?

Various physical and emotional factors can trigger postpartum depression. The most common physical factors include low levels of thyroid hormones, sleep deprivation, inappropriate diet, misuse or abuse of alcohol, and underlying medical problems. There are emotional factors or emotional stressors such as the death of a loved one, recent divorce, social isolation, lack of support, financial troubles, or if your child is experiencing any medical problems.

Possible Treatment

If you notice any of the symptoms discussed in the previous section, you need to immediately consult your doctor. Don't put this visit on hold. Medication and therapy are the two main treatments used for postpartum depression. They can either be used as a stand-alone therapy or as complementary treatments. A mental health specialist can provide you with some medication, or a psychiatrist can offer you counselling.

In addition, practice a strict self-care routine. Once you start taking care of yourself, it should automatically make you feel better about things. From eating a well-balanced diet, getting sufficient rest, and exercise to indulging in your hobbies can help alleviate symptoms of depression. If this does not help, again, consult a professional.

There are some natural supplements you can try to alleviate symptoms of depression, apart from maintaining a proper diet rich in nutrients, with little to no processed foods, and practising meditation and mindfulness. You can also ease the symptoms with sufficient physical exercise and sleep. Taking an omega-3 supplement, spending time in the sun, and including the herb like St. John's wort can be helpful. (Do not take any supplements, or initiate any significant lifestyle changes without consulting a medical professional.)

All these simple steps should be used as a complementary treatment and not the sole cure. Ensure that you follow your doctor's instructions and stick to the treatment as prescribed.

Postpartum Obsessive-Compulsive Disorder

What Is It?

It's quite common for new mothers to experience a variety of emotions once their baby has arrived. There is an increased risk of occurrence, recurrence, or worsening of mood and anxiety-related disorders during the postpartum period. It also increases the risk of postpartum obsessive-compulsive disorder (OCD). Intrusive thoughts or behaviours often characterise this type of postpartum anxiety disorder in response to any perceived dangers the mother might harbour about her baby's well-being. These thoughts or behaviours are often repetitive, constant, and can severely disrupt one's daily life. It's a severe condition that needs immediate medical attention. Women who deal with post-partum OCD are aware of their compulsion or condition but are helpless or powerless to do anything about it.

What are the Common Symptoms?

The most common symptoms manifest themselves as a combination of different obsessions and compulsions. They present themselves in the form of different thoughts and behaviours based on such compulsions and obsessions. Some of the most common obsessions mothers dealing with postpartum OCD experience are; concerns about acciden-tally harming the baby through their own perceived care-lessness, fear of making poor decisions that might harm or fatally injure the baby, or worry that their baby would develop any severe illnesses. They might also be terrified of exposing the baby to toxins perceived as chemicals and other sorts of pollutants.

Other disturbing symptoms of OCD might manifest as unwanted thoughts of images of hurting their baby, such as throwing or dropping him, intrusive thoughts about stab-bing or suffocating the baby, and even unwanted and disturbing thoughts of sexually abusing the baby.

Mothers who suffer from postpartum OCD are often sensitive and hyper-vigilant to anything associated with child abuse. Irrespective of whether it is sexual, physical, or anything else along these lines. Some of the common compulsions a mother with postpartum OCD might experi-ence include refusing to feed the baby because of fear of poisoning him and getting rid of all sharp objects such as scissors and knives. Also, not eating certain foods, or taking medications because she fears she will harm the baby, or even refusing to change the nappy for fear of sexually abusing the child.

Other compulsions include obsessively checking whether the baby is sleeping, consciously and continuously monitoring any thoughts about the baby that are sexually inappropriate, and seeking constant reassurance from others around her to ensure that the baby is not abused or harmed. A mother with postpartum OCD might consciously avoid news articles involving child abuse and obsessively poring over the day's events to ensure that nothing terrible happens to their baby.

Usually, the symptoms of postpartum OCD often show up in the first 2-3 weeks after childbirth. There have been several instances where women haven't noticed the severity of their symptoms. When left unchecked, the symptoms gradually worsen and can be quite damaging because they don't go away on their own.

What are the Probable Causes?

The most common cause for postpartum OCD is believed to be significant changes in critical hormones such as estrogen. Any disruption in the activity of these vital hormones can disrupt the function of essential neurotransmitters in the brain, such as serotonin. Significant disturbances in these hormones and neurotransmitters can result in the development of postpartum OCD. However, from a psychological perspective, it is often due to the overwhelming challenges associated with a baby's arrival that some women cannot deal with. Stress can also be a significant driver for postpartum OCD.

Possible Treatment

As with postpartum depression, postpartum OCD can effectively harm the bond the mother shares with her child. It can also cause pain and suffering to not just the mother, but all the other family members too. If you notice that you're experiencing any of the symptoms associated with OCD, you must seek medical help. The full medical assessment includes a psychiatrist history evaluation and several medical tests to rule out any biological issues such as hypothyroidism, which can manifest as OCD. The most common treatment for OCD is cognitive-behavioural therapy that helps eliminate intrusive and negative thoughts about the baby and his well-being. You might also be prescribed selective serotonin reuptake inhibitors and other medications to reduce the strain on your nervous system.

Postpartum Panic Disorder

What is it?

Postpartum panic disorders are another type of postpartum anxiety disorder. It is a mental health problem that can damage your physical well-being and prevent you from effectively executing your daily functions. This mental health disorder is often characterised by symptoms of excessive fear and worry, which prevent you from functioning effectively. The anxious thoughts you experience can manifest themselves in the form of panic attacks. These panic attacks might be triggered frequently or sporadically. There can be different triggers, but most panic attacks are about worries and fears about the baby's well-being, health, and safety.

What are the Common Symptoms?

The most common symptoms of postpartum panic disorder include trouble concentrating, remembering things, an inability to relax, excessive indecisiveness, being distracted all the time, difficulty completing tasks, insomnia, fatigue, feeling uneasy for prolonged periods, and irritation and agitation, and the loss of appetite. Other factors include suicidal thoughts or any attempts, agoraphobia, avoidance of things out of worry, or fear that something terrible might happen, and panic attacks.

There are three common fears women with postpartum panic disorder experience: fear of death, loss of control, and worrying about going crazy.

What are the Probable Causes?

Doctors are yet to identify the specific cause of postpartum panic disorders. Usually, it's a combination of various risk factors and biological problems that manifest in this mental health condition. As with any other form of postpartum anxiety, this condition may be due to a significant decline in certain hormones' levels. During pregnancy and after childbirth, hormone levels can increase, and the body tries to reduce these levels after the baby is born. If your body fails to do this, it may result in severe changes in your behaviours and mood, which are strong enough to cause emotional distress and anxiety, ultimately manifesting as panic disorders.

Past experiences with anxiety, previous agnostic of panic disorder, traumatic childbirth, thyroid dysfunction, negative childhood experiences, lack of sleep, excessive fatigue, and poor diet are some of the risk factors you should be mindful of.

Possible Treatment

The first step to treat this condition is to acknowledge and accept the symptoms that are harming your well-being. Seek help from a medical health professional if you notice any panic attacks and intense anxiety attacks. The usual course of treatment for this includes cognitive behavioural therapy, medication (for relieving anxiety and mood swings), and various alternative therapies, including nutrition and exercise plans and carefully subscribed supplements.

Taking Care of Yourself

After going through all the information in this section, you'll realise the intricate relationship between your physical and mental well-being. Once you start taking care of yourself physically, the chances of these mental health problems also decrease significantly.

~

Five Things to do if You Feel Overwhelmed as a First-Time Mother

Irrespective of all the time you spend learning about what to expect, motherhood will be quite different. There's nothing that can actually prepare you for what it will be like to be a mother for the first time. Therefore, it is natural to feel a little overwhelmed and stressed. You might have heard a lot of advice about midnight feeding sessions, changing nappies at odd hours, or crying, babies. However, rarely do people talk about dealing with the overwhelming feelings and emotions you might experience. It is crucial to ensure that you stay level-headed and don't allow these emotions to get the better of you. Even if it is a little confusing and scary, it can be adequately handled if you feel overwhelmed. In this section, I will share some tips I have used to take care of myself.

Understand that your emotional and mental well-being

is as important as your physical health. If you don't feel like yourself mentally, it will harm the quality of your life and take the joy out of motherhood. Even when you feel overwhelmed, remind yourself that this is normal, and all mothers experience it. You are not alone, and there is no need to stress, worry, or get anxious about it.

Let's go through a few ideas on how to reduce stress and worry in your life, and find a healthy balance between your personal needs, the needs of your baby, and your family.

Reduce Your House Cleaning Standards and Expectations

Your picture-perfect home might now be scattered with piles of laundry, baby's toys, or even feeding bottles. Well, this is common, and you should learn to accept your new reality. As a new mom, your primary focus would be the health, well-being, and happiness of your little one, as well as your happiness. So, don't worry about the household chores for a while. As long as the house is relatively neat and clean, reduce your house cleaning standards. If you cannot maintain your home like you used to, it is okay. No, you are not a superwoman or a tireless machine. You are human, so stop trying to be a perfectionist.

Ask for help from friends or other family members if you can use a hand when things start feeling overwhelming.

Simplify Your Routine

Learn to simplify your daily routine and declutter your schedule. If there are any tasks or errands that others can take care of, outsource, or delegate the responsibility immediately. Before your baby entered your life, you probably had an elaborate morning routine. You might have spent time deciding your clothes, doing hair and makeup, and so on. After a baby, all such elaborate routines will be baby-centred. From filling her bottles to cleaning them and sanitising her toys and clothes, there is a lot you need to do.

To prevent you from feeling too overwhelmed, here is a piece of simple advice you can use. Learn to prioritise. Think about all the different steps from your pre-mom routine that matter to you and make time for only those things. Prioritising not only frees up a lot of time but also reduces physical and mental strain. If your makeup routine makes you happy and makes you feel more human, then hold on to it. Or maybe you like doing your hair or spend some time reading the newspaper in the morning. Whatever it is, make time for it and skip the rest.

Make Meals Easier

Unless you have a full-time housekeeper, stay-at-home help, or a nanny, it is impossible to cook elaborate meals when you first bring your baby home. Learn to simplify all the meals you consume during the initial couple of weeks following delivery. Stick to this protocol for a couple of months until you've fully recovered. No one expects you to cook a three-course dinner daily. So, stop being hard on yourself. The time you have should be dedicated to taking care of your little one and yourself; this is all that matters. Cut yourself some slack and eliminate all sources of unnecessary stress.

These days, there are various alternatives you can use, such as a meal delivery service. Try to do some batch meal prep whenever possible and opt for batch cooking and one-pot meals. Your partner or other members of the household can also pitch in.

Ask Your Partner, Friend, or Relative for Help

Even a little assistance from your partner, friends, relatives, or other loved ones can make a huge difference. It could be all the difference between sleep deprivation and getting sufficient sleep. Therefore, you don't have to hesitate to ask for help. As a mother of four, I know the most valuable thing during my children's infancy was all the support I got from those around me.

There are also different online support groups that you can join. Talk to your loved ones about it. If you need anything, ask them to help you out. Your circle of friends and family members want to help you and would not mind if you asked them to help you prep some dinners, pick up groceries or do other household chores. If this means getting a break for about 30 minutes, it can do miracles for your physical and mental health.

Learn To Say No

Childbirth is a significant change and a notable milestone in your life. It is also an ordeal in and of itself. Therefore, it is evident that you will need some time to recover from it and get used to the changes you are experiencing. You need to do all this while you are coming to grips with the reality of taking care of the little life you introduced to the world.

Your friends, relatives, acquaintance, and other loved

ones will want to come to drop by for a visit, greet the baby, or visit you. Their intentions might be well-meaning, but it can be physically and mentally tiring for you. You might not be in a position to handle such visits, or even want to socialise. If you feel this, it is okay, and you don't have to feel guilty. Learning to say no, even to the most well-meaning relatives, is essential in being a mother. Learn to be kind and compassionate towards yourself, first and foremost.

If you feel you are not up for a visit, for example, simply say no. You don't have to be considerate about others' feelings because you and your little one's well-being should be your only priority. Gently saying, "Thank you so much, but I'm going to get caught up on some much-needed rest. Can I let you know when might be a better time?"

Time Management

If you want to reduce the stress or anxiety you experience as a new mother, then managing your time is an essential aspect of your life. Time management is necessary not just for new mothers, but for pretty much everyone. There will be a lot to do with a new baby, and at times, it might feel like you can barely keep up and stay afloat. Some moms like to go with the flow, while others like to keep track of everything. Irrespective of which category you fall into, staying organised is essential.

You can maintain a diary or journal to manage your time, but these days, there are a variety of applications you can use to do all this. In this section, I'll share some straightforward tips and tactics with you, and the various mobile apps that will help you stay more organised.

Baby Schedule

During the first couple of weeks, it's essential to track the fundamentals of your baby's activities. From his eating schedule to sleeping patterns and feeding times, making a note of them is crucial. All this information comes in handy whenever you take your baby for his doctor visits. This vital information ensures that your baby is happy and healthy. Suppose you don't like the idea of maintaining a journal to do this. In that case, you can download an app such as the BabyTime app, My Baby & Me, or anything similar (there are many options!) to keep track of your baby's weight, height, feeding times, sleep schedule and so on. These apps will also come in handy if you need to share the responsibilities of taking care of the baby with other household members or hired help.

To-Do Lists

A practical and simple technique you can use to stay on top of all the different things you need to do is create a to-do list. You can include all the various activities, errands, or chores that you have to complete. When you start striking items off this list, it will make you feel better and less anxious.

Since your emotional and mental well-being is significant, I highly recommend that you start maintaining a to-do list. If you know you have ten things you need to complete, it becomes easier to achieve them systematically. A to-do list also helps prioritise different activities and chores you have to complete to pay attention only to the important ones. For instance, after making a to-do list, you might realise some tasks can be efficiently outsourced. If that's the case, delegate them right away. You can use a mobile application such as Microsoft To Do or Todoist to create and share to-do lists with others.

Maintaining the Budget

Welcoming a new member to your family is a joyful occasion, but you need to maintain your budget. The financial implications of a baby are quite profound these days. Unless you learn to deal with it and stay on top of things, you will go overboard. After all, it's not just the present you need to plan for but also your baby's future.

You can use an application, such as Wallet or Monefy, to keep track of your finances. Most of the financial applications available these days allow you to keep track of all the bills payable, expenses incurred, and also establish category-specific budgets. You can link your credit/debit card so that you don't have to remember the credentials whenever you log in or pay for an expense. Even if it seems like a tiresome job, this is a great way to reduce the mental stress you experience. Financial pressure is quite real, and unless you learn to deal with that, it will eat away at your happiness. Financial disagreements are a leading cause of divorce, so getting your financial household in order is imperative for your relationship, as well.

Baby Photographs

I know practically all parents like capturing every moment of their baby's new life and sharing those moments with friends and family. Organising these photos digitally, as well as creating a physical scrapbook, is a great idea. After all, these are precious memories that will stay with you forever. These memories become even more special when you can see them in front of you. These days, there are a variety of applications you can use to do this. For instance, the app FamilyAlbum! It offers a photo book application that allows you to capture, caption, and organise all the important milestones in your baby's life.

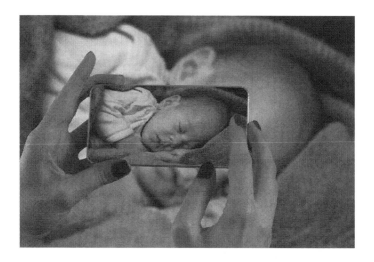

A simple Google search will show you all the different apps you can use to stay organised while taking care of your baby's needs.

If you can manage your time wisely, this activity reduces the stress of motherhood. It ensures that you concentrate on activities that add value to your life while eliminating unnecessary ones. Improving your time management is also a great way to make sure that most of your time is spent taking care of your baby's needs and bonding with him.

Link Between Physical Health and Mental Health

After the birth of your baby, you will feel fatigued for a while. It also takes a couple of weeks before you feel like your usual self. All the regular feeding sessions, nappy changes, late-night feeds, and dealing with a new baby takes up all your time and attention. When you are exhausted, the last thing on your mind might be to exercise. However, if you manage to exercise, it's not just good for your physical health but also your mental health.

When you exercise, your body releases good hormones that help alleviate stress, anxiety, or any other negative thoughts you might have. It's not just a stress buster, but it also is an excellent way to lose all the pregnancy weight you might have put on. If you exercise regularly, even if it is just for 20 minutes, a few times a week, you will soon feel more energetic. If you feel energetic, you will automatically feel better about yourself. Exercise also ensures that you get better sleep at night. All these things are essential for your physical and mental health.

Exercise After a Vaginal Birth

If you had a vaginal birth or a straightforward birth, you could start with a couple of gentle exercises. Do this only if you feel like you are up to it. You can perform simple stretches, walking, or other pelvic floor and tummy exercises to get back in shape. Ideally, you should wait until after the first six-week checkup before you resume any physical activity. Once your GP gives you a clean bill of health, you can start exercising. In fact, after vaginal birth, you are often encouraged to start walking and moving as much as possible. Even if all you do is walk from the kitchen to the bedroom, it helps. If everything is okay after the six-week postnatal check, you can resume high-intensity exercises, such as running or even aerobics. Once the six-week waiting period is up, you can continue gentle exercises.

Walking

The purest form of exercising is walking. If you want, you can place your baby in the stroller and take her for a walk with you. You can start walking in the house and slowly increase the distance. You don't have to run or jog if you don't want to. Start with simple walking and gradually build up the pace until you can briskly walk for up to an hour. Don't overexert yourself and stick to the 20-minute time limit initially.

Gentle Stretches

You can practice breathing exercises, leg and arm circles, Kegels, neck stretches, and leg slides. Do these exercises only when you feel fine, and don't rush into it. Again, wait until the six-week checkup, and consult with your GP before taking on an exercise regime.

Pelvic Floor Muscle Exercises

Simple pelvic floor muscle exercises help strengthen the muscles which control your bladder, vagina, and womb. To prevent incontinence, improve the quality of sex, and reduce the risk of a prolapse, try pelvic floor exercises. You can do these while you are sitting, standing, or even lying down. You can pretty much do them whenever you want. To perform pelvic floor exercise:

1. Breathe in, and draw in your bottom by tightening the muscles in your vagina.
2. Squeeze these muscles as if you're stopping yourself from peeing or like you would during sex.
3. Hold on to this for up to 10 seconds, and slowly relax. You can perform short and long squeezes.
4. Try to perform ten repeats of this exercise at least three times a day.

After a while, your muscles will be stronger than before.

Exercise After a C-Section

If you had a C-section or a complicated birth, then the recovery period will be longer. Before you think about exercising, it is always suggested you should talk to your doctor or midwife. While you are in the hospital after the C-section, you usually get all the information about exercises from the midwife or doctor. If you were used to doing any pelvic floor muscle exercises during your pregnancy, then you can start doing this after the C-section once the catheter is removed. Or, wait until you feel better, and start doing these exercises. You can strengthen the different muscles, which support your bladder, bowel, and womb with pelvic floor exercises.

After the prenatal checkup, if the doctor or the midwife says you can start exercising, start immediately. Once again, it is entirely up to you, and there is no fixed timeline you need to follow. If you don't think you're up to it or don't want to, then take some more time and start when you are fully ready.

After a C-section, you might need to wait for at least 12 weeks before resuming any high impact exercises such as weight training, aerobics, or running. You can slowly increase the workouts' intensity once you have recovered from the C-section, and there is no pain or discomfort. Start with low impact exercises such as jogging, low resistance jumbo, swimming, yoga, or even Pilates.

5

CRYING AND HOW TO SUCCESSFULLY COPE WITH IT

I had a new mother reach out because she had trouble dealing with her baby's crying. She asked me, "How do I make my baby stop crying? I feel like I have tried everything, but nothing seems to be working. What can I do? At times, I start questioning my parenting skills!"

There was a point when I asked myself the same questions she was asking me now. Even you might be thinking about what you can do to get your baby to stop crying.

When Your Baby is Crying

It can be a little tricky to deal with a crying, upset, or a colicky baby. Learning to calm, soothe, and comfort your infant, while staying calm yourself, is essential. In this section, you will learn about straightforward tips and tricks

you can try to soothe and comfort your baby and successfully cope with his crying.

Possible Reasons Why the Baby Cries

Babies often cry to communicate their needs. It is the
only form of communication he knows until he starts talking. There are different reasons why a baby cries, and you
need to learn to respond to his cues. It can be a little tricky
to understand why he cries, especially if he doesn't stop
crying. You might start worrying something is wrong with
him, lose your calm, or even question your parenting skills.

When I was a new mother, there were instances when I
thought I could not connect with my daughter, and that's
why she was crying. However, let me reassure you, you will
eventually get the hang of it. You are new to motherhood, so
don't be too hard on yourself if your baby doesn't stop
crying.

One of the common reasons your baby cries is because

it's her only way to capture your attention and express her needs. Understanding your baby's cries can be a little difficult to interpret initially. However, once you start spending time with your little one, you will learn to differentiate between her cries. The way she cries when she is hungry will differ from her cries when in any physical discomfort. Once you become attuned to her needs and recognize why she cries, it becomes easier to soothe her.

Babies usually cry when they are hungry, sleepy, or tired, or have wet or soiled their nappies. Excessive stimulation from noise or activity around him can also cause overstimulation that prompts them to cry. Food allergies, colic, acid reflux are also common causes. Other reasons she might cry are any pain or illness, anxiety, fear, or gas trouble.

Dr Harvey's 5 S's for Soothing a Crying Baby

Paediatrician Harvey Karp came up with five uncomplicated actions to soothe your baby, especially if it seems like he's crying for no apparent reason. These five tips are dubbed as the five S's, which will help soothe your crying baby by creating a safe and secure environment that's reminiscent of his time spent in your womb. The five S's are swaddling, shushing, swinging, sucking, and the side of the stomach position.

You can swaddle your baby in a comfortable blanket to make sure that he feels secure. Hold your baby, such that he is always lying on his side of the stomach when awake. Make sure that he still goes to sleep while on his back. These positions are quite comforting and will make him feel safe. Another simplistic way to soothe a crying baby is by swinging him in a slight rhythmic motion. You can take your baby for a ride in the car or a stroller, or gently sway while cradling him in your arms. To soothe a crying baby, you can offer a pacifier or shush him slowly. The white noise created by a fan, white noise machine, vacuum cleaner, or even a hairdryer helps drown any background noises, making him feel secure. Another option is to play white noise videos on YouTube or any other streaming platform.

<u>What to Do if the 5 S's Don't Work</u>

In most cases, the five simple tips mentioned in the previous section will help. However, there are times when these won't work. If so, here are other suggestions you can use to soothe your crying baby.

If your baby doesn't stop crying, you might need to consider any problem he might have. Not getting sufficient milk to drink, excess stimulation or any other physical discomfort are the obvious reasons why your baby cries. There can be other medical causes for his crying, such as stomach acid reflux, intolerance to the milk he is drinking, or urinary infections. Another possibility, you need to consider is if you are doing the 5 S's properly or not. If these techniques don't work out, then it might be because your technique is a little rusty, or you need to learn to do it properly. These techniques take practice, so stick with them, and be patient with yourself.

Never Shake a Baby

Babies usually cry to communicate their needs or wants. Your baby might cry if he needs your attention, to show he is upset, or keep crying until you respond to his needs. At times, a baby might not cry, and instead tunes out and does not show any emotion. It essentially means the baby becomes unresponsive. If you take a moment and think about it, most adults also tend to do this whenever faced with difficulty. It might seem that taking care of an unresponsive baby is relatively easy because they seem agreeable and quiet. However, suppose your baby doesn't respond to you, external stimulants, or their environment. In that case, you should immediately call your health visitor or GP. If you feel, instinctively, that something is seriously wrong, make a trip to your local A&E. This all depends on the time though. Suppose your GP is closed and you can't get into contact with your health visitor. In that case, the only option is to call emergency services where they would give you advice on whether going to A&E is the right option depending on your concerns and problems. But like I said just above this, listen to your instincts.

Irrespective of what you do, there is one thing you should never do: shake your baby. Even if he seems unresponsive, resist the urge to shake him. If you shake him, it might result in shaken baby syndrome. In this condition, the blood vessels in a baby's head can break because of the impact of shaking. It can also result in brain damage, blindness, seizures, or even mental retardation. Even if you feel frustrated or angry that you cannot prevent your baby from crying or stop his crying, don't shake him. Many deaths occur every year from the shaken baby syndrome.

How to Recognize and Cope with Colic

No two adults are alike, and the same stands true for babies as well. Some babies might sleep through the night, while others cry nonstop. You might hear some parents talk about how easy it was to get their baby to sleep through the night.

As a mother, here is one piece of advice that I want you to follow - resist the temptation of making comparisons. Even if you have a challenging baby, avoid comparisons, and don't have any expectations. If you do these things, dealing with a baby comes more challenging than it already is.

According to doctors, colic is a condition wherein repeated episodes of inconsolable or excessive crying that last for at least three hours daily occur at least three times a week, for at least three weeks in a normally healthy and well-cared for baby. It usually occurs in the first three months of your baby's life. You don't have to worry too much because of a colicky baby. There is no single cure for colic because the definitive cause of it is difficult to determine. Most babies tend to suffer from it at one point or another.

Here are the common symptoms of a colicky baby:

- The baby might cry as if she's in physical pain
- Sudden onset of excessive crying
- Whenever he cries, he clenches his fists, stiffens his limbs, and tightens his stomach

It can be quite stressful dealing with a colicky baby, and here are some tips I know will come in handy.

While dealing with a colicky baby, the first thing you need to do is understand your limits. As a parent, you might believe there are no limits to which you can go to take care of your child. Yes, this is true. However, you should also understand your personal boundaries. Pay attention to your internal warning signs that tell you are reaching your threshold. If you feel overwhelmed, ask for help, step outside for a while, talk to your loved ones, or take a break.

These small steps ensure you are in the right frame of mind while taking care of your baby. Don't hesitate to ask for help, and ask your loved ones, partner, or anyone else to pitch in when you need support.

Babies do cry, and that crying hits a peak when they are around six weeks old. With time, this crying reduces. Therefore, it is not a reason to become anxious or worried. Since time is on your side, take it easy. It might feel like there is no end to his crying, but with a little effort, time, love, and patience, things will get easier.

Parenting is not about perfection. Lose this attitude when it comes to life. If you keep expecting or demanding perfection from yourself, it will merely overwhelm you. No parent knows what to do in every situation. You can try your best, but that's about it. Cut yourself some slack and learn the ropes as you go along. If not immediately, eventually, you will figure things out. So, don't just be patient with your infant, but with yourself, too.

Creative Ways to Soothe a Crying Baby

Music

Music can help soothe a crying baby. You don't have to limit yourself to lullabies or soothing music but can try different genres. You can also play the kind of music you like. If you have watched the famous sitcom FRIENDS, you might recall an episode where Ross sings an inappropriate song to make his daughter smile and giggle. Well, you can try it too!

Music is believed to calm your baby's nervous system, reduce his heart rate, and respiratory rate. You don't have to be a singer to sing songs to your little one. Never underestimate the power of your voice on the baby. Infants find it soothing when their mom sings to them. The familiarity of your voice and rhythm of the music will calm down a crying baby.

Replay Baby's Cries

Another innovative technique you can use to calm your baby is to record her whenever she fusses or cries. The next time she starts crying, replay this soundtrack to her. Chances are, she'll be quite fascinated by the sound of a crying baby. At times, babies can become distressed and have a tough time calming themselves down, even when the problem has been eliminated. When your baby listens to her voice while crying, it acts as a surprising distraction and can help break the crying cycle.

Reduce Overstimulation

Babies often cry when they are overstimulated. Start by reducing the lights in your baby's environment. It could be something as simple as bright lights in her room. Ensure that the room is completely darkened, as it becomes easier to calm a crying baby. Understand that newborns are used to the quiet confines of their mother's womb before they were born. By replicating a similar environment, it reduces the over-stimulation and calms them down.

White Noise

Turning on the white noise, like the sound produced by a fan, or a white noise machine, can be quite soothing to your baby. It drowns out any unpleasant background noises that were probably distracting your little one. It is believed that white noise imitates the sounds an infant hears while in his mother's womb. In a way, it creates a safe and secure environment that is familiar to your baby.

Why you, the Mommy may Cry

A newborn's cry can get anyone's attention, and it is quite overwhelming for a new mother. This cry can be gut-wrenching, which triggers you to drop everything you're doing and immediately tend to your child. There is another thing in which no one tells you or prepares you concerning crying. Your baby's cry can make you cry, but there are other reasons too. After every pregnancy I went through, there were instances when I used to cry, as if on cue. I was oblivious to why I was crying, so I made a list of different reasons I used to cry; I think it will help you.

Happiness

You can cry because you're happy. There were instances when all I needed to do was merely look into my baby's eyes, and the next thing I knew, I was crying. Not just crying, but I used to bawl my eyes out. Maybe you held your baby in your arms for the first time, saw her giggle, or anything else that caused a happy feeling. Even if it seems like a trivial reason, you might start crying. There are times when I cried because I felt so thrilled and overcome with emotions, and all I was doing was cradling my little one in my arms. Prepare yourself for the roller coaster ride of emotions you will be on as a new mother. The highs of it are incredibly blissful, but the lows are something you need to be able to deal with as well.

Tiredness

You probably are used to a hectic lifestyle, but you don't know what tired means until you deal with a newborn. New mothers automatically assume their babies will sleep through the day. Yes, babies sleep a lot, but they also need to be continuously fed, and they poop a lot. Tending to your baby's needs becomes your priority, and every time you see your baby, your maternal instincts kick in. Taking care of a baby is a rewarding job, but it is incredibly tiring too. It can be so tiring that you start crying because of it. Even if it sounds absurd, this is quite true. There were times when my baby and I were both simultaneously crying at odd hours. It happens, and you simply need to deal with it - it's okay.

Breastfeeding Issues

Different parenting magazines might make it seem like breastfeeding a baby is relatively easy. After all, how difficult can it be? All you need to do is encourage your baby to latch onto the nipple, and that's about it. It does take a while to get the hang of it, and even longer if there are any other issues and you don't have the necessary support. You might cry because your nipples hurt or because you're scared you're not producing sufficient milk for your baby or any other issues associated with breastfeeding. You might also cry because he is crying.

Hormones

Do you remember the mood swings you experienced during pregnancy? Prepare yourself because these hormonal changes don't go away the minute you give birth to your little one. It takes your body a couple of weeks to adjust to the changes and get back to its original self. All those hormones that made you go a little crazy during the pregnancy will be back with a vengeance. Since your hormones are calibrating and trying to find some balance, mood swings are frequent. After this, the nursing hormones kick in, and they can also do a number on your mood. These are all small costs to pay for the miracle of birth. If you feel too stressed or tired, take a break and get some rest. At this point is where your support system steps into the picture. So, don't hesitate to lean on your loved ones during this period.

For no Apparent Reason

You might also cry for no apparent reason. Yes, there will be times when you cry for no reason, and it can be quite confusing. It might even make you wonder if you are experiencing postpartum baby blues. This is just normal, and once again, it goes back to a combination of all the factors mentioned earlier. Simple things can make you cry. If you're prepared to deal with it, it becomes easier to make yourself feel better. Once you become a mother, you'll experience a variety of emotions you didn't know existed. All these dormant emotions start to rise to the surface and can make you emotional. Take some deep breaths, and exhale any worries and fears away.

Worries or Anxiety

After you give birth, your only priority will be taking care of your baby's needs and ensuring she is happy and healthy. After a while, be prepared for reality hitting you; that this baby will be in your life, and for the rest of your life. You might start continually worrying about different things you are or are not doing. Anxiety and worries are common. However, if left to their own devices, they can become a little overwhelming and get your tear ducts rolling.

You might be worried about swaddling your baby, have questions about breastfeeding, or your child's sleeping patterns. All this is common, and all new moms experience these fears. However, you don't have to worry too much about these things because all the information you need is covered in this book. Whenever you feel uncertain about anything related to your baby's health or well-being, don't hesitate to call your GP, loved ones, or anyone else you can think of to help.

Moving Past Crying

Now that you're aware of why you can cry, you will not feel something is wrong with you the next time you may start crying. Don't let anyone tell you that it isn't normal for a new mother to cry. After all, your body underwent a lot, and there are several hormonal changes you are trying to keep up with.

6

HOW TO GIVE YOUR BABY A BATH

Our baby is due in just a few weeks! This is our first baby, and we're pretty nervous and very excited to bring her home. I haven't had a tone of experience with infants, much less newborns, so I'm a little apprehensive about how to hold and handle her. I'm also getting a lot of different advice on how to bathe, how often, and what to use. Do you have any advice that will help us?

- Abigail

G iving your baby her first bath might not sound like a major task. Well, new mama, it certainly is! From questions about holding your baby to bathing him, there is a lot to learn. You might be quite anxious about giving your baby's first bath. You might not yet be completely comfortable handling this little person, and covering her body in water might feel extremely strange. With practice, you'll be able to sponge bath her and bathe her. I was quite anxious too! However, with a little guidance and practice, I soon got the hang of it. In this section, I will share with you some tips I used while bathing my babies.

When to Give Your Newborn a Bath

Babies are usually given a bath within a couple of hours of their birth, typically by the midwives if you gave birth in a hospital. Usually, it is recommended to wait until 24-hours to bathe a newborn. This delay helps regulate his blood sugar, body temperature, and also promotes mother-baby bonding. It also ensures that the baby's skin doesn't dry out.

You don't have to bathe your baby daily, and all you need to do is merely clean his face, hands, neck, and the nappy area daily. Washing him three times a week is fine. Your baby is ready to be moved into his bathtub once his umbilical cord stump comes off. This usually takes 5-15 days. Stick to using a baby washcloth with your hands for cleanups, especially if your baby's umbilical cord stump isn't fully healed or is still intact. The same holds true if his (circumcised) penis isn't fully healed. You can always talk to your health visitor if you have any doubts or to get individual advice on when it is okay to move your baby to the bath tub.

Where to Give Your Newborn a Bath

The first few times you bathe your baby, you might feel a little scared about holding him. As long as you keep a firm hold on him and don't allow him to flail a lot in the bath, you don't have to worry. During the first few attempts, you can ask someone to help you fetch anything if you have forgotten some of the supplies. It takes a little practice and confidence to handle a wet, slippery, and wriggling baby. Rest easy as you and your baby will soon get used to a bath time routine and will probably come to enjoy it.

The simplest way to bathe your baby would be in the kitchen sink or a small baby bath in the first couple of weeks. You can use a big tub like the one you may have in your bathroom, but it can be a little awkward because you'll have to kneel and lean over. If you just had surgery, this becomes incredibly difficult. Don't forget to use bath support if you use a big tub. Never leave your baby alone, even if it's just for a second while you bathe. This might sound like a scary fact, but babies can drown in as little as 2 inches of water. So, be alert and extremely careful and vigilant.

How to "Top and Tail" Safely

An efficient alternative to giving your baby a full bath is to "top and tail." This technique helps keep your baby's skin clean. Mothers can top and tail their infants daily, irrespective of their age. It is often used as the go-to alternative for a full-body bath, especially for extremely young babies. In this section, let's look at simple tips to effectively and safely top and tail your baby.

Gather All Supplies

Babies tend to rapidly lose their body heat, so ensure the room is warm at around 24 C (75 F). To top and tail your baby, you'll need:

1. A baby bath or a basin filled with lukewarm water (37 C, 97 F).
2. A large and soft towel
3. Cotton pads or a soft washcloth
4. Clean clothing
5. A nappy
6. Receiving blanket
7. Nappy cream and powder
8. A soft-bristled brush (optional)

Offer Some Reassurance

Before you start top and tail your baby, it is time to offer a little reassurance. Offering comforting words, cooing gently in your baby's ears, or telling him everything is alright, will make him feel safe and secure. Once you have offered reassurance, slowly undress your baby, but let his nappy stay. Now, securely wrap him in a towel.

Wash Around the Eyes

Now, it is time to wash your baby's skin gently. Hold her head in your hand and gently clean the area around each ear with a cotton pad or a cotton washcloth soaked in warm water. Cotton pads are the best option since they don't shed any lint. Gently wipe from the inside corner of the baby's eye and move outward. If there is no dried mucus, then you don't have to wash his eye area.

Wipe the Baby's Face

Use the cotton pad and gently wipe the area around your baby's mouth, nose, and work outwards from the centre until you have covered his entire face. Don't forget to concentrate on the areas under the chin, all creases of skin around his neck, and the area behind his ears. Never put any water in his ear or the nose canal. Gently pat him dry once you've completed this step.

Baby's Hair

You don't necessarily have to wash your baby's head daily, washing it every alternate day is fine. (Before you use any hair cleanser or body wash, talk to your health visitor or GP about it. Use these products as per the directions of the doctor or midwife.) Don't unwrap your baby from her towel. Place your arm behind her back such that your hands gently cup her head. Use your free hand to wet your baby's head with a damp washcloth and apply any cleanser, if suggested by the doctor. If not, merely wash it with some water and let it dry. While you do this, gently massage his entire head, including the fontanelle. This is the area where the baby's skull isn't fully formed yet. Be extremely gentle while you touch it. A simple head massage helps stimulate blood flow to your baby's brain and can be incredibly relaxing for her.

Nappy Area

Never forget to clean your baby's nappy area daily. This is one practice you cannot afford to overlook. Irrespective of whether you sponge bathes him daily or not, clean the nappy area. Use the towel's corner to keep your baby's head, and upper body area covered while you remove his nappy. Wash this area with lukewarm water and gently cleanse him. Wipe your baby's nappy area in a front and back motion.

Afterwards

After you followed all the previous steps, it is essential to ensure you pat your baby dry. Be thorough while you do this, and don't let any wet spots stay behind. As mentioned, babies tend to lose their body temperature rather quickly. Afterwards, you can use gentle baby lotion to moisturize your baby's skin. Wrap your baby in his receiving blanket and dress him up. After, you can spend a little time cuddling with your baby.

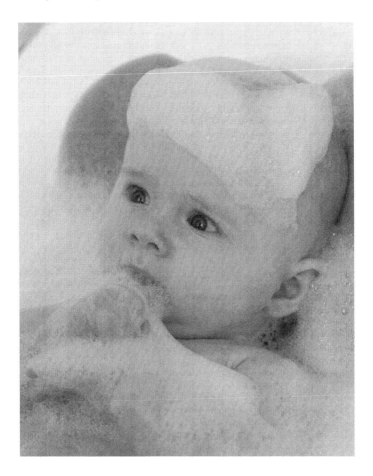

How to Safely Bathe Your Newborn

You don't have to bathe your baby daily, but if he seems to enjoy it, there is no reason you should abstain from it. Avoid washing your baby after his feed, when he is hungry, or tired. While bathing, ensure the room is warm. Gather all the supplies you need to bathe, such as the baby bath or the washing-up bowl with clean and warm water, clean clothes, towels, clean nappy, and some cotton pads or wool. Here are some tips you should keep in mind to ensure that you bathe your baby safely.

Before you bathe the baby, ensure the water is luke-warm. It should be warm and not hot. A simple way to test it is to dip your wrist or elbow in the water to ensure that it is of the right temperature. Also, don't forget to mix the water around to avoid any hot patches.

For the first month, don't use any liquid cleansers in the bathwater and clean only with regular water. If you use soap or shampoo, always consult your GP and/or health visitor and use the products they prescribe.

While your baby faces you, gently clean her face. Next, wash her hair with clean water, while supporting it above the baby bath bowl.

Use one hand to support your baby's head and shoul-ders while gently lowering the baby bath with the other hand. Always keep her head above the water and gently swish the water over her with the other hand.

Remember! Never leave your baby unattended while bathing her, even if it is just for the blink of an eye.

Once you bathe your baby, gently lift her and gently pat her dry. Ensure that you pay special attention to all the creases on her skin, and don't leave any skin wet. After this, ensure that you quickly apply some lotion to avoid drying of her skin.

You can also gently massage your baby to help her relax and sleep. Don't use any lotions or oils until he's at least a month old.

If you notice that she is scared or frightened of bathing, you can try bathing together. While you do this, the water shouldn't be hot, and it is always easier if someone else holds your baby while you get in and out of the water.

The Benefits of Bathing Your Baby

Parent-Baby Bonding Time

A significant advantage of bathing your baby is that it gives you a chance to bond with him. This could be a reason why it becomes a highlight of your day. This time spent together is precious. You get to learn a lot about your baby when you start bathing him. From his tickle spots to his wide-eyed amazement, you can be witness to it all. Be gentle and careful while you clean him. It lets him know he is truly loved. You can coo sweet nothings in his ears, sing some songs, or lovingly gaze into his eyes. A couple of gentle touches and the sound of your voice will make him feel secure and comfortable.

A Learning Experience for the Baby

It might sound incredulous, but there is a lot your baby can learn while in the tub. You can tickle his senses by trickling water gently onto his feet, or tummy. He might giggle with pleasure. You can also give a quick lesson in cause-and-effect by encouraging him to kick the water, which creates a subsequent splash. Watch your baby's wide-eyed amazement when he hears the water as you pour it next to him. As long as your baby enjoys all this and has a good time bathing, there is no reason why you shouldn't do it often. As you watch, you can start naming his body parts as you pat them. If not now, eventually, it will help him learn different things.

Talking to your baby, in all complete sentences, also helps increase their vocabulary. As you're washing him, you can describe what you're doing, in a loving tone so that he will learn new words faster. Plus, he loves the sounds of a warm and caring voice, as we all do.

Helps Soothe Fussy Babies

Do you ever feel better after taking a bath, especially when you feel tired, irritated, or cranky? Well, this is pretty much what your baby also experiences. Soaking in a tub after a long or a tiring day is quite therapeutic, calming, and comforting. To further your baby's relaxation, you can gently massage her. Most babies often love it, but if she starts to fuss or turns her head around, you don't have to worry. You will soon figure out something she likes. If this doesn't work, you can try cuddling with her after bathing her. It will undoubtedly help soothe her, especially if she's fussy.

Prompts Better Sleep

Another advantage of bathing your little one is that you can easily add to his bedtime routine. The warm water, the feeling of being safe and secure, the touch of a loving mother, and the warm water will magically put your baby to sleep.

7

DEVELOPMENTAL MILESTONES TO EXPECT FOR THE FIRST 24 MONTHS

My health visitor told me that our six-month-old baby is doing just fine. But I've noticed that my sister's baby, who is just about the same age, seems to be more advanced with her physical strength. But this is my first baby, and I'm not sure what to expect. My sister has had three babies, and she told me that everything is fine. I guess I'm just worried that my baby will fall behind as he gets older.

- Gail

There are different developmental milestones babies hit within their first 18 months. Many new moms are not aware of these development milestones and, therefore, don't know what to expect. A developmental milestone doesn't mean it's your baby's birthday. Instead, it involves activities that babies usually start performing or behaviours they display at a certain age.

Trust me, over the next 18 months, your baby will learn

so much, and watching him grow will be an incredible experience for you. From his first smile to when he starts to hold his head up, starts crawling, and walking, everything is a developmental milestone. Once you know what to expect, it becomes easier to ensure that your baby is healthy and grows at an age-appropriate rate.

Note: Don't forget that all babies are unique, and some develop in different ways and at a different pace. However, if your baby is well behind a typical milestone, or if you ever feel concerned, speak to your health visitor and/or GP to ensure your baby is developing like he is supposed to.

First 3 Months

By the time your baby is three months old, you'll notice he is beginning to develop a sense of things around him and is developing his sense of touch. It means he is slowly becoming aware of the world around him. The best way to assist him is by exposing him to the textures of different materials. Add some touch to enhance his overall experiences.

Your baby's head will probably be wobbly during the first couple of weeks, and her movements will be jerky and sudden. However, she will slowly be able to lift her head and chest while lying on her stomach. She might even try to kick her legs in this position. Your baby might also start grasping and holding on to any objects that you give her. Her motor skills will slowly develop.

By the time babies are two months old, they can start making different cooing sounds. Even if it sounds like your baby is gurgling, it is her way of trying to communicate with you. She might try repeating the vowel sounds whenever you talk to her.

During this period, your baby's vision is also slowly developing. When babies are 3-months old, they usually like bold patterns in high contrast, both colours or in black-and-white. By this time, his vision becomes more coordinated, and he can slowly track the movement of different objects. Soon, your baby can recognize familiar people and even objects at a distance.

If Something Isn't Right

It is quite reasonable if your baby manages to reach some developmental milestones ahead of schedule while she lags in others. Since babies tend to develop at their own pace, it isn't something you can rush irrespective of what you wish to happen. However, it would be prudent to be aware of the different warning signs of any developmental delay. If you're concerned about your baby's development or notice any of the red flags discussed in this section when she is three months old, immediately call your GP or health visitor.

- An inability to move control her head
- No response to external stimuli, such as sounds, the sound of your voice, or people around her
- An inability to grasp hold on to objects
- Cannot follow moving objects with her eyes
- The baby doesn't notice her hands

As mentioned, babies tend to develop at their own pace, but it doesn't mean you should start ignoring your instincts.

The sooner you detect a problem, and the more effective the chosen treatment would be.

4-6 Months

Your baby's motor skills are slowly evolving and strengthening at this age. He can probably wiggle and kick his arms and legs more purposefully. He will also try to rock on his stomach and rollover. His ability to control the movements of his head also increases as his muscle strength develops. At this age, most babies can easily raise their head even while lying face down. By the time babies hit the six-month mark, they slowly try to push themselves up by shifting their weight down to their legs and trying to get up.

During this stage, babies can easily hold on to objects and are good at grasping them. From a finger to a rattle or any other soft object, your baby can hold on to it with a secure grip. Also, keep in mind that anything that is well within your baby's reach will eventually end up in his mouth. Therefore, new mamas, be careful about any small objects lying around the house and in baby's reach.

Your baby might also start babbling different noises and other sounds. She concentrated mostly on the vowel sounds until she was three months old, but now, even the consonants matter. She probably uses her voice to express her joy. Your baby can also differentiate different emotions based on your tone. By this age, most babies can even recognize the sound of their names.

Your baby's vision also starts to improve and develop. He can now effectively differentiate between shades of reds, yellows, and blues. He might also like intricate patterns and will start noticing his reflection and the colours of his toys.

7-9 Months

When you review your baby's milestones, ensure that you consider her overall behaviour to judge the progress she makes. Also, ensure you adjust for prematurity. Therefore, talk to the health visitor or GP if your child misses any developmental milestones. Since every child develops differently, missing one or two milestones shouldn't cause any significant concern. However, if she misses major milestones, consult a doctor at the earliest indication of a problem.

By the time your baby is about 7-9 months old, she should be doing the following things.

- Your baby can sit without any support and can reach for toys without falling over.
- While lying on her tummy, she can lift her head and push her body weight on her elbows without any difficulty.
- She can start to move her arms and legs alternately, and begins to creep and crawl slowly.
- She can easily move from sitting by herself to rolling on her tummy and vice versa.
- Her vision becomes better and can effectively track objects, even while she is sitting.
- By this age, babies often try imitating others around them.
- Your baby starts to show more control while sitting and rolling.
- She can effectively pick up small objects using her fingers and thumbs instead of just grabbing onto them as she did earlier.

If your baby cannot sustain her weight on her legs, doesn't transfer toys from one hand to another, uses only one side of her body to make any movements, uses only one hand predominantly, or does not use her arms properly while sitting. It might be a good idea to talk to your health visitor and/or GP about it.

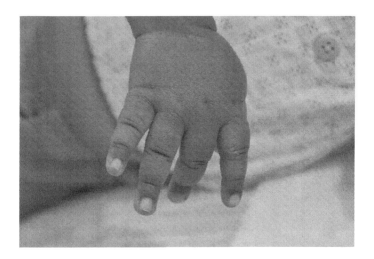

10-12 Months

By this age, your baby can clasp his hands, release objects or toys into a container with a bigger opening, and pick up small items using his thumb and pointer fingers. He can also pull himself to a standing position and start cruising around the room, using the support of furniture or anything else in the surroundings. He can stand alone and take several independent steps and maintain his balance whenever he is sitting or throwing any objects. At this age, babies can also easily move in and out of different positions to get the things they desire or to explore their environment.

If you notice your baby only uses one of his arms to shift his weight while standing, has any difficulty standing on his legs because of stiffness or pointed toes. Or sits with all his weight only on one side, only uses the support of his hands to sit, or doesn't have proper control to hold his head in an upright position, talk to your health visitor or GP about it.

13-18 Months

By this age, babies can walk independently and don't often fall, can squat to pick up toys or other objects, and can start stacking blocks or other items.

Suppose you notice your baby cannot walk independently, walks on her toes, doesn't have proper balance while standing, falls frequently, cannot crawl, uses a pincer grasp to hold on to objects, or cannot pull herself to a standing position. In that case, you should talk to your GP and explain this.

19-24 Months

By the time your baby is 21-months old, he can use up to 50 words, can imitate new words he picks up from others, identify about 3-5 body parts, name objects in pictures, understand simple pronouns such as "me," "my," and "you," and can grasp new words quickly.

Once your baby hits the 24-month mark, he can use two-word phrases, will start listening to stories, understands the meaning of action words, and can also use gestures and words for playing. Apart from this, he can also follow simple directions. As long as there are only two steps involved, such as "pick up the toy and bring it to me," for example.

Keeping Track

Now that you're aware of the different developmental mile-stones, you should look out for them, as they give you an idea of whether your baby's development is on track. This also ensures you can take corrective action immediately in case of any developmental difficulties or lagging abilities. Whenever you are worried, don't forget to call up your GP. At times, babies take a while longer to develop, and it is okay. Some babies might start sitting and standing earlier than others, while others might be able to talk sooner. Bottom line is don't worry if your baby misses a milestone or two along the way. Sooner or later, most babies catch up.

After the birth of my first child, I was quite anxious about all these developmental milestones. I often sought reassurance to ensure my baby was fine. Well, if you do this, don't worry because you aren't alone. However, learn to manage your emotions and expectations. If you cannot control these things, it will strain the bond you share with your little one, and cause undue stress.

Enjoy watching your baby grow up, and take in all the fun moments, and the joy of being a mom.

8

HOW TO IMPROVE YOUR NEWBORN'S BRAIN POWER

Our daughter is a year old, and at first, we thought everything was great. Honestly, I'm not sure if things are normal, or 'off.' I guess I'm looking for some advice and information. For example, my neighbour's one-year-old uses words and hand signals to tell her parents what she wants, but my daughter just uses her hands and noises. I do notice that my daughter loves reading time, and knows some of the different words in the book. Is there something I can do to make sure she has the skills she needs when she starts school?

- Tanya

A common question I get from many concerned and anxious new mothers is what they can do to aid their baby's brainpower. The early years of childhood play a critical role in your baby's brain development. The brain not only develops into a fully functional

HENRIETTA MULLINS

major organ but starts forming different neural networks too.

At the time of birth, the average baby's brain's size is about the quarter of an average adult's brain. This size doubles up within a year. It tends to grow to about 80% of the adult size by the time a baby is three years old and is almost fully developed by the time he turns five. The human brain is an incredibly powerful organ and is the seat of control. A newborn baby has all the neurons that will stay with him for the rest of his life, but the connections between these cells make the brain work. These connections enable us to talk, think, move, and do just about anything else. Therefore, childhood years are incredibly crucial for the development of his brain and the formation of neural connections.

Possible Ways to Improve Your Newborn's Brain Power

Choose Toys that Allow Your Baby to Explore and Interact

We all love to buy toys for babies. These days, there are a variety of toys available. However, instead of selecting toys that look cute and pleasing, opt for ones that allow your baby to explore and interact. Simple toys such as stackable blocks, shape sorter activities, or pop-up storybooks help your child understand simple cause and effect relationships.

For instance, if a child starts to stack too many blocks without proper alignment, it will stumble and fall. The next time, if he stacks the blocks properly, they will stay in place, and this is the simplest way in which children can learn.

Respond Promptly When Your Baby Cries

The limbic area of the brain is responsible for processing and understanding our emotions. When you

98

promptly respond to your child by cuddling, soothing, reassuring, and nurturing him, it creates positive brain circuitry in this crucial area. If your baby starts crying or is fussy, try cuddling him or hold him in your arms. It not only reassures him and makes him feel safe and secure, but it also develops a positive bond with him. This emotional security he experiences is vital for his mental development.

Give Your Baby a Body Massage

Giving body massages to babies, not only makes them feel relaxed and calm, but also enhances their overall sense of well-being, and makes them feel secure and loved. This kind of loving touch promotes emotional and physical growth in babies. It is also a simple way in which you can learn what your baby likes and doesn't.

Encourage an Early Passion for Books

Babies love colourful images and high contrast pictures. Select books that are filled with plenty of big pictures that are colourful and bright. If you start fostering your baby's love for books from an early age, this habit will stay with him forever. While your baby points at the images, join in his delight. If possible, try making appropriate sounds or noises that correspond with the book. For instance, if there is an image of a cow in the book, then you can moo or bark if it's a dog. Learn to modulate your tone while you read to him and encourage your toddler to talk about books. This activity aims to increase your baby's receptive language, or his understanding of the words you speak, instead of concentrating on his expressive language (what he says) during infancy.

Baby Talk

We often talk to babies in a high-pitched tone we don't use with adults. Well, this kind of baby talk is quite rewarding for your baby's mental development. So, engage in a lot of baby talk. Whenever your baby coos or gurgle, reply in delighted vocalizations while slowly drawing out your syllables in a high-pitched tone. Talking like this is known as 'parentese.' couple this with exaggerated happy facial expressions and drawn-out vowels will help your baby absorb the different sounds, language, in which you speak to him. The different areas of your baby's brain that are responsible for recognizing and understanding speech and language reproduction will benefit from this rich input.

Play Games that Involve Hands

Different activities like "this little piggy," "patty cake," puppets, or even peekaboo help capture your baby's attention and engage her. When you use your hands while interacting with babies or kids, it teaches them how to interact with the physical world. Not just the words, but your baby picks up on your physical cues as well. Therefore, hands-on activities should be included in your daily routine if you want to improve your baby's brainpower. These are fun activities, enjoyable for mom and baby and dad and baby.

Alternative Ways to Improve Your Newborn's Brain Power

All parents wish for a happy and healthy baby. After all, what more could we want? If I'm honest, most of us secretly hope that our little bundle of joy will grow up to be a genius. I know mothers who played Mozart to their bellies while pregnant or decorated the nurseries with stimulating shapes and colours. Many parents make a common mistake to offer TV and other gadgets as a way of entertaining their babies. Well, this isn't the best way to go about boosting your baby's brainpower. This section will show you some more rich and exciting ways to support your baby's brain development.

Gentle Roughhousing

Gentle roughhousing, or pure physical play, is quite essential for your baby's growth and development. It could be something like tickling his toes or using a feather to tickle his belly. This kind of physical play improves his cognitive functioning.

Joyful Playtime

We all love approval, encouragement, and compliments. Well, babies are no different. Instead of allowing your child to play by himself, spend some time with him and see what he does. Even if it is something as simple as stacking one block on top of the other, offer encouragement whenever he does something good. It shows your baby that what he is doing is right and that you approve.

Suppose you want your child to become an enthusiastic and actively engaged learner. In that case, it is crucial to help develop sufficient dopamine levels in his brain. Dopamine is a feel-good chemical that encourages positive feelings. The simplest way to do this is by spending more time playing games at his level and offering encouragement.

Storytime

Perhaps the most effective and straightforward way of teaching your baby empathy and emotional vocabulary is via storytime. The sooner you start, the more effective and easier it will be for your baby to understand all these things later in life. Are you wondering how all this works? Well, it's not just about reading a story to your little one but concentrating on identifying and labelling the different emotions the characters might be experiencing at various points in the story. Eventually, it encourages children to view things from others' perspectives, not just their own. For instance, if a person, animal, and any other character in your child's picture storybook isn't experiencing a happy moment, then mention it, or ask them what they think the character is feeling.

Exploration

It is relatively easy to hand a toy to your baby and allow her to engage in solo play. However, it would do you both some good to find activities that you can engage with your baby. It not only provides time for mother and child bonding, but it also is an excellent way of learning more about your baby.

Try to add some sensory and stimulating items to playtimes, such as a box filled with feathers, playing with bubbles, or anything else that your baby would love. One-on-one human interaction is perhaps the best way to teach your baby something new. When you hand your baby a new toy, give him a couple of minutes to explore it, by himself. After this, jump in and teach him how he can use it better.

Irrespective of whether your baby turns out to be whip-smart, these tips will certainly offer his tiny brain the support it needs during these very formative years.

Other Ways to Improve Your Newborn's Brain Power

Stimulating Baby's Vision

Newborns don't open their eyes frequently, but when they do, make the most of such brief moments. Look into her eyes, and spend some time gazing at her. Babies can recognize faces from an early age, and since your face is one of the most important ones, she will see, let it stay in her memory.

Stimulating your baby's vision is an uncomplicated way to develop her brainpower. Allow your baby to look at her reflection in the mirror, or show her similar pictures with small differences. All these things encourage her to think, using visual cues. Even a two-day-old infant can imitate simple facial expressions of those around her.

Read Books, Again and Again

Babies as young as eight months can recognize a sequence of words in the story if you read the book a few times in a row. Therefore, make a point to read books again and again with your little one. Even if it's the same story, repeat it a couple of times, and your baby will soon catch on. This is the simplest way to teach him a new language and encourage him to learn.

If there is a specific story your baby likes, then you can

replace the main character's name with his. Repetition is the best way to help your toddler learn.

Teach Texture

Teaching textures is also a fun activity that helps improve a baby's brainpower. If she likes to pull tissues from a box, then let her. All it costs are a couple of pounds, and you have a sensory plaything your baby can crumple or smooth out. You can also hide a couple of small toys under the tissues, and as she pulls the tissues out, she can discover these toys and feel elated.

Grab a box and fill it with pieces of different fabrics such as silk, wool, cotton, linen, or even terry cloth. Take a piece of cloth and run it along your baby's body, across his tummy, along the length of his feet, or even on his cheek. Let him understand the different textures; this is a great way to increase his sense of touch. While you do this, describe how each of these fabrics feels. For instance, if you are running a soft piece of cotton on his tummy, you can say something along the lines of, "look how soft it feels!" If you sound excited about it and talk in a high-pitch, your baby will be excited too.

Play and Be Silly

As a mother, you get a rare opportunity to relive your childhood and grow with your baby. So, don't hesitate to play and act a little silly at times. You can play peekaboo with your little one, and he will start to giggle within no time. It teaches your baby that objects can disappear and reappear! Surprise your baby with a couple of unexpected kisses, hugs, cuddles, or even by gently blowing on his tummy. You can blow raspberries on his belly and listen to his giggles or laughter. There is nothing more precious than a baby's wholehearted laugh.

Exploring New Surroundings

Place your baby in a stroller or a baby sling and take her for walks. While you walk, start describing the surroundings to her. This is a simple activity where mothers and babies can bond together while exploring new surroundings. Start narrating all that you can see. For instance, if you notice a puppy playing in the park, tell your baby, "there is a puppy playing," or "look at the flower." This is an effortless opportunity to teach your baby new vocabulary.

Whenever you need a break or need to get some shopping done, take your baby with you. The different environment of a supermarket, and various new faces, and colours your baby can see will be quite stimulating for her. A simple change of scenery can work wonders for a baby.

Bonding

Bonding is critical not just to your baby's development and growth, but also for your relationship. Irrespective of how you feed your baby, make the feeding time entertaining and engaging. You can sing songs, hum tunes, or simply talk to him in a loving voice.

Try to limit your baby's screen time as much as you possibly can. Instead, concentrate on one-on-one interactions for his brain growth. For instance, whenever you change your baby's nappy, use this time to teach him about different parts of his body. Narrate different body parts you touch while you move them around. The World Health Organisation guidelines recommend that screen time is not recommended from infants to the age of 2 and that 'engaging in reading and storytelling...is encouraged'. Dr Juana Willumsen, one of the guideline authors, states that 'Sedentary time should be made into quality time. Reading a book with your child, for example, can help them develop their language skills'.

Spend at least a couple of minutes daily, "doing nothing" with him. Simply sit with him. Get rid of all distractions, and focus all your attention on him, and enjoy this time.

9

COMMON WORRIES AS A FIRST-TIME MOTHER AND HOW TO GET THROUGH THEM

Oh my gosh, I'm so nervous about having our first baby. Don't get me wrong. My partner and I are elated and excited. We've got his nursery all set up. We have been having fun picking out blankies, decorations, infant clothes and learning toys. It's amazing. But sometimes I'm lying awake at night, worried about if I'm going to be a good mom. We both want to be the best parents we can be. Are we worrying too much?

- Elisabeth

I was wrought with worry after the birth of my first child. I had many questions, doubts, and concerns about things I was and wasn't supposed to do. I used to get anxious even when my baby sneezed. Once I spoke to other mothers, I realized most of the worries I had were common, and I wasn't alone. This section looks at some typical concerns all new moms have and tips to deal with them.

Your Newborn's Poop Color

You would've probably never even imagined all the time you will spend observing your baby's poop. Yes, observing your baby's poop will become a priority and a regular activity for you. It might not sound pleasant, but this is the only way to determine whether your baby is getting sufficient food and if he is well or not. After all, nothing will come out of the bottom unless he's had something from the top. Some babies tend to poop whenever they eat, and most breastfed babies tend to poop at least three times a day.

Let's take a look at what the colour of your baby's poop signifies.

Meconium is a black and sticky substance that tends to collect in the lower bowel, pooped out after birth. The baby's first bowel movement will be black, and this is nothing to be worried about. It usually happens on the first or the second day after he is born. Call the doctor immediately if he doesn't poop more than once in the first two days, or if there are black stools on the third day. By the third day, a healthy baby's poop will be green or yellow. If the poop is still black on the third day or if he poops less than three times within those three days, then it can be a sign that your baby is not getting enough to eat.

If your baby is breastfed, then the poop will be yellow or brown on the fifth day. If he is formula fed, the poop will be yellow, grainy and seedy. You can expect at least three of these storiesools daily by the fifth day. When compared with breastfed babies, the colour, consistency, and smell of formula-fed babies are different and such babies tend to have fewer bowel movements.

Call your GP and health visitor immediately if his poop is red, black, white, or clay-coloured. These different coloured poops are often signs of an allergy or an infection in the upper intestinal tract or even symptoms of any liver or gallbladder issues.

It is a sign of severe dehydration if you notice dark-coloured pee or reddish stains in your baby's nappy.

When Your Newborn Sneezes

If your baby starts to sneeze suddenly, it's probably not a problem. Babies sneeze because it's the only way in which they can clear their nasal passage. Airborne particles often get stuck in his respiratory passages; to get rid of them, he starts to sneeze. It also helps your baby reopen any temporarily blocked nostrils that happen when he is pressed up against you while feeding. If he sneezes after feeding, it means his body is merely trying to reopen one of his blocked nostrils.

Your baby will need medical attention if he has a fever, runny nose, congested breathing, or has any trouble breathing. Unless these things happen, you don't have to worry if he starts to sneeze.

Being Perfect

No one is perfect, and no one can be perfect. However, many new mothers tend to spend a lot of their time worrying about all things that can go wrong or if they are doing something incorrectly. They are worried about harming the baby unknowingly. The common mistake they make while doing this is, they start to compare themselves with others and forget that every baby is unique. Instead of spending all your time worrying about all these things, concentrate on deciding what works for you. Irrespective of how terrific a mother you are, you cannot do everything by yourself. Instead of aiming for perfection, try to do your best, and it will be more than enough.

Scared that You Won't Bond with Your Baby

Another common fear that new mothers have is worrying whether the baby will bond with them. Even if you don't feel all warm and fuzzy for the first few weeks after your baby is born, it's quite reasonable. You can blame all this on the hormones that are running wild in your body.

Here is a little secret I'll share with you. Your baby starts to bond with you when he is in your uterus. He listens to your heartbeat and voice. Within his first week, he can recognize your distinct smell and will crave your company. A simple way to bond with your baby is to offer skin-to-skin contact. Hold him with you as frequently as you can and engage in many fun activities together. Even if you don't feel an instant connection with your baby in the delivery room, you need to stop worrying. You will develop a one-on-one connection with your little one in no time.

How Much Sleep Does a Baby Need?

As with adults, sleeping patterns and requirements of babies and children are quite different. Some babies need more sleep, while others do well with less. A newborn baby can sleep anywhere between 8-18 hours daily. Once your baby is about 3-6 months old, he will need to sleep for eight hours or a little longer at night. For babies between 6-12 months, night feedings will become obsolete, and they can sleep for up to 12 hours at night. In general, as your baby grows, the duration of his sleep at night will slowly increase.

Unsure of how to keep the umbilical cord clean

The area around the umbilical cord stump is what needs to be cleaned and hygienic. The best time to clean this area could be when your changing nappies. Firstly always wash your hands before and after cleaning it. To do this, you can wet cotton wool with warm water to gently clean the area around the umbilical cord stump. The umbilical cord stump itself doesn't need cleaning unless it's stained with urine or poo. If so, just use water to wash it off. Contact your midwife or health visitor for guidance and advice as keeping the umbilical cord clean and dry is vital if you want to avoid infections. Signs of infections are:

- Reddening and swelling of the skin around the stump
- a foul smell from the base of the stump
- Your baby crying if you touch the stump
- Bleeding from the base of the stump

If you see any of these signs, call your health visitor and/or GP as soon as possible.

Note: If you want a video on umbilical cord care, the NHS website has a fantastic video made by midwives to visually assist you.

Illnesses and Your Baby

New mothers often worry about any illnesses their baby might have. The thought of your child becoming sick is gut-wrenching. I have had these worries, several times and had many sleepless nights. After a while, I learned to trust my instincts.

At times, it might be a little challenging to determine whether your baby is ill or not. In such instances, go with your gut. You know your baby better than anyone else, so give yourself a break. If her behaviour or appearance seems a little worrying to you, you can consult your health visitor or GP about it.

If your baby has difficulty breathing, makes any noise while breathing, and breathing is rapid along with high or low body temperature, it could be a sign of an illness. If your child continually cries and you cannot do anything to console her, or if her cry doesn't sound normal to you; if her vomit is green coloured, or her skin starts losing its colour, then these are some red flags you should not ignore.

Worried About Sleeping Dangers

SIDS (sudden infant death syndrome) is extremely rare, but it's a significant concern for most new parents. Even though it is rare, there are some tips you can use to diminish the risk almost entirely. Ensure your baby always sleeps on his back and isn't wearing any restrictive clothing while sleeping. Another thing you need to ensure is to avoid keeping pillows, bumpers, thick blankets, or any stuffed animals in your baby's crib.

Worried About Dropping the Baby

Relax and breathe a little while handling your little bundle of joy. If you are worried, start baby proofing the entire house to prevent accidental tripping over any objects and falling. Ensure there are no snags on the rugs or the carpets around the house and keep all sharp objects away from the steps. While you are holding your baby and walking, take your time and don't be in a rush. Secure your baby by cradling him in your arms whenever you move around with him, and be mindful of your steps.

10

DON'T FORGET YOUR PARTNER OR YOUR MARRIAGE

I'm a little embarrassed to write this, but I have a lot of concerns about my sex life with my partner. Before I got pregnant, we had a great sex life, but now I'm not interested at all. I'm worried that I'll never want sex, again - and, it's such an essential part of our relationship. Is what I'm feeling normal? Will I get my libido back?
    - Sharon

A common fear that many new mothers harbour is about their personal life and their relationships: welcoming a baby into your life is a significant change, and it will change a lot of your relationships too. However, there is one relationship you shouldn't forget about, and it is the one with your partner. Never ignore your partner (or your marriage). Remember, you are both a team and are in it together.

When I say this, I am speaking from experience. My partner was my rock and my pillar of strength through all my pregnancies. Parenthood becomes more comfortable and inherently more manageable when you have a partner to rely and depend on. So, don't make the mistake of ignoring this vital relationship. In this chapter, I will share with you some practical and straightforward tips that will help your marriage or relationship. From making time for each other to rediscovering the romance in the bedroom, you will learn a lot in this chapter.

Keep Your Relationship on Track

Take a Walk Down Memory Lane

Spend time with your partner and take a stroll down your memory lane. You can go to the park for a walk, drive around for a bit, or even just chat aimlessly. If you want, you both can talk about the different things that made you fall in love with each other. Reminiscing about these things will undoubtedly rekindle the spark in your relationship.

Small Gestures

Love isn't about making grand gestures all the time. In fact, in a long-term relationship, all that matters are the small things. It could be something as simple as a note that says, "I love you!" on the fridge, or breakfast in bed, that can put a smile on your partner's face. A couple of unexpected kisses, cuddling, or even leaving love notes, can make a lot of difference about how you both feel. It will also make you feel closer than ever before.

Involve Your Partner

Your maternal instincts might prompt you to try to do

everything associated with your baby by yourself. But, it's not just you who needs to bond with the baby; your partner needs to do this too. Working together as a team can bring new parents closer. Encourage your partner to feed and bathe the baby. This also gives you a respite from your daily duties, so that you can unwind and relax.

Support and Encourage

Never forget to support and encourage each other. You should be able to count on your partner and vice versa. Be there for each other. After all, you both have a baby to care for now. If there are any problems one of you faces, then talk about it. Listen to each other's worries and issues and have an open discussion about it. Even if you cannot solve your partner's problems, you can at least lend an ear, listen, or offer a shoulder to lean on.

Spend Time Together

Spend a little time with your partner. Even if it is only for 20 minutes; ensure that you both spend time with each other. Talk about your daily lives, feelings, or even any worries. During these 20 minutes, get rid of all distractions and concentrate only on each other.

Communicate

Every healthy relationship is based on honest communication. If you cannot talk to your partner openly and honestly about your worries and dreams, then something is probably lacking. Therefore, ensure that there is no scope for miscommunication by keeping the channels of communication open between the two of you. Life will become more pleasant if you have a partner you can share everything with.

Don't Forget About Sex

Intimacy often takes a backseat after pregnancy. You should prepare yourself for some changes in your sex life once you step into the role of a parent. Dealing with sex and intimacy is often a challenge for new parents. You now have less time; there are more hormonal changes to deal with, you're always tired, and probably have several worries about contraception.

All these things can make a simple and pleasurable activity feel quite scary and daunting. Change can be scary, but it isn't necessarily bad. If it feels like things have started to cool down in the bedroom, it's merely a sign that you should start concentrating on the relationship with your partner. Trust me; things will get back on track. In the meantime, you need to be a little patient with yourself and your partner. A straightforward way to do this is by not forgetting about your sex life. In this section, I'll answer some frequent and general questions many new mothers commonly ask me.

How Long to Wait

A lot about your body will change after pregnancy and delivery. One thing that is not immune to such change is your sex life. After delivery, various hormonal changes take place in your body that make you more sensitive and make the vagina tissue thinned. It also takes some time for your vagina, cervix, and uterus to return to their usual size. Breastfeeding can also reduce your libido in general. In a nutshell, your body will need some time to recover after delivery, and it will be a while before you can start thinking about sex again.

As such, there isn't a specific timeline you can follow to determine how long you should wait before you want to have sex. Usually, doctors suggest you need to wait for anywhere between 4-6 weeks before engaging in sexual intercourse after a vaginal delivery. Resume sexual activities only after getting a clean bill of health from your midwife, GP or gynaecologist.

Apart from physical recovery, understand that welcoming a new member to your family means a lack of sleep and a drastic change in your routine. If there are any perineal tears, or if an episiotomy was performed, then it will take a while longer to recover from it all. Suppose you rush into it and don't give your body the time it needs to recover. It increases the risk of unnecessary complications such as a postpartum haemorrhage.

Because of fluctuating hormone levels, you might not experience any sexual desire in the weeks following the delivery. With time, everything gets better. In the meantime, learn to be patient with yourself and talk about all these things with your partner. If you have any doubts about it, consult your midwife, GP or gynaecologist.

Advice for Healthy Postpartum Sex

A baby is not the end of your sex life. Let's take a look at some tips that can help you - I know they helped me!

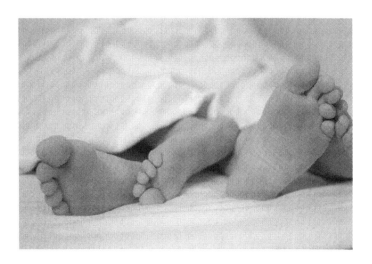

Make Time for Sex

I know having a baby at home changes your life and lifestyle. You and your partner might not have a lot of time for spontaneity, with a new baby at home. However, if you make a conscious effort and work together, you can come up with some time for fun sex. If you do this, neither of you will feel rushed or anxious about the activity. Unless you make time for it, it will become challenging to maintain a healthy postpartum sex life.

Practice Kegels

A common post-delivery issue that many women suffer from is incontinence and weak vaginal muscles - both of these can negatively affect sex. Kegel exercises are not only simple to perform, but you can pretty much do them anywhere. Kegels not only help your vaginal muscles' stamina, but they also help your vagina regain its sensitivity to stimulation.

Talking with Your Partner

Let go of any inhibitions you have about your body. Unless you do this, you will feel anxious and apprehensive about doing anything in the bedroom. Just because your body is different, doesn't mean sex cannot be fun or exciting. To do this, you should always maintain an honest and open dialogue with your partner. If you have any worries, talk about it. When you share your fears, you might realise your partner has particular concerns too. The best way to ease this discomfort that you each feel is by communicating. You can also talk about the different things that feel good (or not), so sex becomes more enjoyable.

Play with Foreplay

Foreplay can be quite a turn on by itself. At times, you might not want to do anything more than engaging in a little foreplay. Never underestimate the power of foreplay when it comes to sex. Foreplay can make sexual intercourse incredibly pleasurable. Foreplay also increases the natural lubrication secreted by your vagina. If you aren't quite ready for penetrative sex, you can try mutual masturbation or engage in other types of sexual activities.

Use Lubricant

Never shy away from using a lubricant if your vagina isn't able to produce the necessary lubrication. Sex without lubrication can be and will be painful and uncomfortable for you and your partner. To avoid all this, use lube. Don't use an oil-based lubricant because it can rupture condoms and increase the chance of vaginal irritation. Instead, opt for a water-based lubricant. If you have any doubts about it, you can talk to a gynaecologist.

Take it Slow

Sex doesn't have to be a rushed activity. Take your time and take it slow. During the first few weeks after your baby is home, you might not be in any state to jump right into the sheets. Honestly, it's okay if you feel that way. Even in the first few weeks after your doctor clears you for sexual intercourse, you might not be physically or mentally ready to jump right back to your pre-pregnancy activities.

Learn to take things one day at a time, and it will get more comfortable. If you don't feel comfortable about doing something, then talk to your partner about it. You can start by taking leisurely baths or showers together, giving each other massages, or even cuddling. You are the only one who can decide what you wish to do. Don't let anyone else tell you otherwise, and certainly don't feel pressured to start having sex again.

One thing you must always remember is that intimacy

isn't about sex. Even simple acts of spending time together with your partner help rekindle the romance in your relationship. Spend time together, have open and honest discussions, and take things slowly. Remember, there is no rush, and you can set your own pace together.

11

THINGS GET BETTER!

Our toddler, Joshua, is just about two-years-old. Of course, we love him like crazy - he's funny and loving. As new parents, though, we still feel overwhelmed, even as Joshua is becoming more and more independent. I don't think we're used to, still, not having the freedom that we once had, even though we're happy to have this new family. We're considering having another baby, but we're concerned that a second child will completely take over our lives. Some of our friends have several children, and they seem happy, even with all the mayhem. Can that be us, someday?

*   - Nancy*

The initial years of motherhood, especially your baby's first two years, may be the most joyous and exhilarating years of your life and will also be an endless marathon of tiredness and exhaustion. There will be times when you start wondering if things will ever go back to being "normal." Dear new mom, I know it can be scary at times, but I promise it will get better. Things will get better and more relaxed.

The first time I dropped my child in year 1, I couldn't believe she was already five years old. The five years leading up to that moment in time were filled with endless precious moments. I still remember my baby's first cry and how much I struggled as a new mother. However, with a little practice, patience, and compassion, things got easier.

I came to this simple realisation - the only thing that mattered was my attitude. The reality of parenthood is quite different from all the pre-baby daydreams you might have indulged in. It is also quite different from the glossy pictures featured in parenting magazines. However, it is quite beautiful in its own way. From holding your baby in your arms for the first time to watching him grow; every moment is overwhelmingly beautiful and joyous.

Irrespective of all the parenting books you read, and the advice you receive from other moms, it cannot prepare you for the experience you have, unless you live through it. In this section, I'll teach you some simple tips you can use to enhance your experience of motherhood and change your overall attitude.

Your Attitude Matters

In life, all that matters is your attitude. The right attitude doesn't mean you have to smile when you don't want to. Instead, it means changing your internal thinking and rewiring your brain to look at the positive side of every situation. Your attitude matters a lot because it influences how you experience motherhood. Here are three simple ways in which you can change your attitude for the better.

Don't Compare Your Baby to Another

Never make the mistake of comparing your baby to another. Every baby is unique, and your bundle of joy is wholesomely unique. If your GP says your baby's weight is fine, then trust that. As long as he eats, sleeps, and doesn't seem unwell, there is no point in over-analysing how much to feed him or wonder if he's as big as your neighbour's baby.

Don't Compare Yourself to Anyone Else

Instead of comparing yourself with others, and feeling worse, it is better to concentrate on yourself. If there are things you enjoy doing, then make time for that. If wearing good clothes and doing up your hair suits you, then go for it. If you feel better after painting or exercising, then engage in those activities. You are the only one who can determine what you need to do and how you should feel.

Don't let anyone else make you feel bad about your feelings.

You are not like other mothers, and your baby is unique. Comparison tends to breed unhappiness, and nothing else. Instead of going down that path, learn to concentrate on yourself. You can be awesome doing what you want to do, and live life the way you want.

This is an essential piece of advice for all aspects of your life and not just motherhood. Once you let go of the unnecessary desire to compare yourself with others, you will instantly feel better about yourself.

Take Care of Yourself

Yes, you have a baby at home, but it doesn't mean it's an excuse for neglecting yourself. Learn to take care of yourself, and you can be a better mother to your baby and feel much better about yourself. If you don't take care of yourself, you will soon be exhausted, overwhelmed, and tired beyond measure. Once you start taking care of yourself, you will automatically feel better about motherhood. Take some time to meditate, exercise and partake in activities that you love. Ask a family member or your partner to watch the baby for a few hours so you can go shopping for some new clothes, or just get out of the house and pamper yourself for a little bit of time.

Adjust Your Goals

The day you have today with your child will never come again. He will still be your baby tomorrow, but he will be a day older. Therefore, learn to live in the moment and stay in the present if you want to enjoy motherhood. Don't go through the motions of motherhood without mindfulness. Learn to take joy in the little things of life, and the time you spend with your baby will become more meaningful.

Learn to adjust your agenda, and life will get easier. I often felt incredibly overwhelmed by motherhood when I didn't manage to accomplish these agendas. As a new mother, it is time you accept the simple reality that life will be a little hectic until your baby grows. Until then, learn to lower your expectations and redefine what a productive day means to you. For instance, spending 20 minutes singing lullabies to your baby might make you feel productive. If that's the case, then go ahead and do it! It is essential to plan and prepare, but if you get too involved in these activities, you will forget about the present. "Right now" is what's most important, sometimes.

After all, your past cannot be changed, and the future cannot be predicted. Therefore, make the most of the moment you have right now. Step away from your lengthy to-do list, and concentrate on your baby's laughter. The sound of laughter that's filled with joy and genuine delight will undoubtedly make you feel a lot better.

The Truth About Motherhood

There will be times when motherhood feels quite lonely. This feeling of loneliness sets in soon after you bring your baby home, especially once all the visitors stop dropping by to see the new baby. If you feel alone and lonely, talk to your partner and other loved ones about it. If this doesn't help, there are a variety of new mother support groups you can attend. If you thought you were not the sort who would want to participate in meetings at a support group, think again. There is no harm in reaching out to others who are experiencing the same thing you are.

Most mothers often view their babies as a reflection of

themselves. Unfortunately, it isn't fair for you or your baby. Your baby is not you, and he does not represent you. If he cries a lot or doesn't want to sleep, it doesn't mean you are a terrible parent. If he doesn't want to listen to the stories you tell him, it is not a reflection of your parenting skills. It merely means your baby is not ready for it. If one method doesn't work, there are different techniques you can try.

Your maternal instincts will almost always be spot-on. If something seems off or just not right about your baby, then don't ignore your instinct. Whenever in doubt, go with your instincts. If you are worried about something your baby does, it's always better to take him to the GP. Even if it means everything was fine, you may at least stop worrying.

You might be quite excited about documenting and photographing every single thing your baby does. The good news is, these days, most phones and cameras come with a lot of storage space. If you don't want these memories to get lost in that space, it is better to start printing things as you go along.

Maintain a Positive Mindset

There will be moments when it feels like you will never get a good night's rest, your pre-pregnancy body, or anything else along these lines. Well, in such instances, remind your-self that this too shall pass. In life, nothing is constant, and the only constant thing is change. Therefore, maintain a positive mindset about it and change becomes more natural. Whenever you feel like this, remember that you can trust yourself and your baby. You are not the only one going through these things, and it is reasonable to feel all the varied emotions that you do. Instead of getting overwhelmed, you can learn to deal with it by having a positive mindset. Everything you feel is a part of a normal and healthy experience in motherhood.

Have a little patience, and surrender your expectations. Believe that things will work out the way they are supposed to. Everything is a part of a process, and don't be in a hurry to reach the end of the story. Forget about everything you heard from other mothers about being the perfect mother. Let go of those stories and accept that you are who you are right now. You can change for the better, learn new things, and become a better mother. However, stop chasing the mirage of perfection.

You are enough, you are okay, and you are doing a fantastic job. Remind yourself of this simple mantra whenever you feel a little low. Whenever you see your infant's face and the small smile on it, remind yourself you're doing a good job. No guidebook will give you the exact steps you need to follow to raise a child. It is a learning process, and the learning curve is rather steep. If you're willing to learn, then everything will be an enjoyable experience. Therefore, work on maintaining a positive mindset and discover the joys of motherhood.

CONCLUSION

"Motherhood: All love begins and ends there."
- Robert Browning

Prepare yourself for the biggest adventure of your life! Once you step into the role of a parent, your life will never be the same again. This is one of the best changes you will ever experience. The joys of motherhood are unlike any other.

As promised, in this book, you discovered plenty of tips, tricks, and techniques you can use to deal with your worries and anxieties as a new mother, and take care of your baby to the best of your abilities. We all need a little help from time to time, and new mothers need it more than anyone. As a new mama, enjoy the joys of motherhood, and it will indeed be rewarding.

Whenever in doubt, reach out to your support system for help, and refer to the information in this book. Taking care of your little one will come instinctively to you, and it isn't something you need to worry too much about. As a mother of four kids, and someone who made plenty of mistakes along the way, I hope this book will be quite helpful while you embrace your role as a mother.

All the tips, tricks, and strategies that are given in this book are tried and tested by other mums and me. I know they will help ease your transition into motherhood and improve your confidence as a new mum. With this information, you can go through the most magical period of your life without it being overshadowed by unnecessary worries, fears, or doubts.

There is one thing you should never forget, and that is to love yourself, your baby, and your new life. Loving your baby will come to you naturally, but don't forget about yourself in this process. Understand that you have everything to gain and nothing to lose by experiencing the joys of motherhood. While you do this, don't forget to take care of yourself! You are not only responsible for your child's well-being, but yours too. No one else can do it for you.

Put all your fears and worries to rest and use the simple yet helpful information given in this book to ease yourself into motherhood.

Enjoy!

REFERENCES

Arsenault, A. (2017, January). How Can I Stay Organized as a New Mom? Retrieved from www.thebump.com website: https://www.thebump.com/a/how-to-stay-organized-as-a-new-mom

Arsenault, A. (2017, January). How Can I Stay Organized as a New Mom? Retrieved from www.thebump.com website: https://www.thebump.com/a/how-to-stay-organized-as-a-new-mom

Breastfeeding Problems. National Institute for Health and Care Excellence. (2017, May). Retrieved from cks.nice.org.uk website: https://cks.nice.org.uk/topics/breast-feeding-problems/management/breastfeeding-problems-management/

Brain Development - First Things First. (2018). Retrieved from First Things First website: https://www.firstthingsfirst.org/early-childhood-matters/brain-development/

Cassidy, A. (2020, March 20). 100 essential tips for first-time parents (from mums who've been there). Retrieved from IMAGE.ie website: https://www.image.ie/life/baby-board-100-essential-tips-first-time-parents-mums-whove-127846

Thrush, Breastfeeding Challenges, Start4Life – National Health Services. (2021). Retrieved from www.nhs.uk website: https://www.nhs.uk/start4life/baby/breastfeeding/breast-feeding-challenges/thrush/

Dineen, C. (2020, January 28). 6 Genius Ways to Make a Baby Stop Crying. Retrieved from Parents website: https://www.parents.com/baby/care/crying/ways-to-soothe-a-crying-baby/

Bleeding After Birth – National Health Service. (2018). Retrieved from the www.nhs.uk website: https://www.nhs.uk/pregnancy/labour-and-birth/after-the-birth/early-days

Diproperzio, L. (n.d.). 10 Things New Moms Shouldn't Worry About. Retrieved from Parents website: https://www.parents.com/baby/new-parent/motherhood/10-things-new-moms-shouldnt-worry-about/

Goyal, N. (2018, July 30). 43 Best Foods to Increase Breast-milk Supply Quickly in 2020. Retrieved from Being Happy Mom website: https://www.beinghappymom.com/foods-increase-breast-milk-supply/

Holland, K. (2019, March 22). Sex After Birth: What to Expect and How Long to Wait. Retrieved from Healthline website: https://www.healthline.com/health/pregnancy/sex-after-birth

World Health Organization. (2019, April 24). To grow up healthy, children need to sit less and play more. Retrieved from who.int website: https://www.who.int/news/item/24-04-2019-to-grow-up-healthy-children-need-to-sit-less-and-play-more

Growth Development. (n.d.). Retrieved from Pathways.org website: https://pathways.org/growth-development/

How to Top & Tail Your Baby. (n.d.). JOHNSON'S® Baby UK website: https://www.johnsonsbaby.co.uk/bath/top-and-tailing

Karp, H. (n.d.). What to Do If the 5 S's Aren't Calming Cries. Retrieved from Happiest Baby website: https://www.happiestbaby.com/blogs/baby/5-ss-arent-working

Toilet Stool – The Ohio State University Wexner Medical Center. (2018, January 9). Retrieved from Wexner Medical website: https://wexnermedical.osu.edu/media-room/pressreleaselisting/toilet-stool-mmr

Kelly, O. (2019). Strange Obsessions After Birth Can Be Due to Postpartum OCD. Retrieved from Verywell Mind website: https://www.verywellmind.com/postpartum-obsessive-compulsive-disorder-2510665

Kloss, K. (2019). 20 Ways to Boost Your Baby's Brain Power. Retrieved from Scholastic.com website: https://www.scholastic.com/parents/family-life/creativity-and-critical-thinking/learning-skills-for-kids/20-ways-to-boost-your-babys-brain-power.html

Mahak Arora. (2019, August 16). 16 Advantages and Disadvantages of Bottle Feeding. Retrieved from FirstCry Parenting website: https://parenting.firstcry.com/articles/bottle-feeding-advantages-and-disadvantages/

Major, M. (2018, July 16). Here's the Scoop on Your First Post-Labor Poop. Retrieved from Healthline website: https://www.healthline.com/health/parenting/first-bowel-movement-after-labor

Melinda. (2018, November 2). HelpGuide.org. Retrieved from HelpGuide.org website: https://www.helpguide.org/

articles/parenting-family/when-your-baby-wont-stop-crying.htm

Michelle Roberts. (2019, April 24). No Sedentary Screen Time for Babies, WHO says. Retrieved from BBC News Online website: https://www.bbc.com/news/health-48021224

Pampers. (2020, August 14). Taking Care of Your Baby's Umbilical Cord. Retrieved from pampers.co.uk website: https://www.pampers.co.uk/newborn-baby/care/article/newborn-umbilical-cord-care

O'Connor, M. (2020, March 10). Have Varicose Veins? Retrieved from What to Expect website: https://www.whattoexpect.com/pregnancy/symptoms-and-solutions/varicose-veins.aspx

Watson, S. (2015, June 10). C-Section: Tips for a Fast Recovery. Retrieved from Healthline website: https://www.healthline.com/health/pregnancy/c-section-tips-for-fast-recovery

Printed in Great Britain
by Amazon